D1202705

Prickly
Roses

stories from a life

Prickly
Roses

stories from a life

First Edition 2017
Published in the United States of America
Printed by Spencer Printing
ISBN 978-0-9969726-5-9

Publisher's Cataloging-In-Publication Data
(Prepared by The Donohue Group, Inc.)

Names: Abell, Joyce.
Title: Prickly roses : stories from a life / Joyce Abell.
Description: First edition. | Baltimore, MD : Passager Books, 2017.
Identifiers: ISBN 978-0-9969726-5-9
Subjects: LCSH: Abell, Joyce. | LCGFT: Essays. | Humor. | Autobiographies.
Classification: LCC PS3601.B45 Z46 2017 | DDC 814/.6--dc23

Passager Books is in residence in the Klein Family School
of Communications Design at the University of Baltimore.

Passager Books
1420 North Charles Street
Baltimore, Maryland 21201
www.passagerbooks.com

Prickly
Roses

stories from a life
Joyce Abell

Joyce Abell (signature)

Passager Books
Baltimore, MD
2017
passager

To my son, Crispin Sartwell
and my grandchildren
Emma, Sam and Jane Sartwell

Memory is the mind's own theater.

Octavio Paz

Prickly Roses

Little Girl Tossed

It was the fall of 1928, I was three and a half years old, and my parents and I lived in New York City. That was the year my mother's father gave my parents a marvelous gift – his two-year-old Buick automobile. My parents, Hilda and Murray Gitlin, both 25, became giddy with their possibilities. Both had graduated from college: my father from Columbia University, my mother from Barnard

College. After graduation, my father made a little money sporadically working at a restaurant; my mother worked as a salesgirl at Macy's. Poor as they were, once they owned a car, they joyously schemed toward adventure, deciding to give up their jobs and their apartment to spend several months – maybe a whole year! – wandering around the country, with our ultimate destination being the opposite of New York City: New Orleans.

My father, an aspiring but not yet published writer who hoped to become America's 20th-century Walt Whitman, yearned for this odyssey because he believed that anyone who wanted to call himself a great American writer first had to understand "the heart of America" – its farmers and factory workers, its Negroes and its poor. My mother was ready for adventure anytime and almost anywhere: her heart was that of a gypsy, without emotional ties to any place or anyone.

To support the three of us, they intended to offer their services at farmhouses along the way and assumed that, as we drove farther south toward our destination, there would surely be work picking cotton or vegetables or something. My muscular, handsome father had, in fact, a great deal of experience on his family's Connecticut farm with cows, cornfields and vegetable gardens. My slender, more worldly mother, on the other hand, had been raised by upper-middle-class city folk and had probably never even thought to nurture plants, whether for food, beauty or anything else. But she was whipsaw smart, sure of herself and a quick learner.

Early in the first morning of our adventure, my mother packed the Buick with food enough for at least a week – a giant salami, a huge chunk of Swiss cheese, loaves of rye bread, apples, water. She set me on top of a suitcase with several blankets for cushioning, so I would be able to watch the changing view out the windows. Next to me was a pile of picture books when I got tired of that. And off we went.

Finding work turned out not quite as easy as they had thought it would be, farmers being just a wee bit suspicious of strangers from New York leaping from an elegant Buick to declare themselves hard-working, competent farmhands, looking only for free room and board. All too often we slept in our car, my father on the front seat, my mother on the back seat and me on the floor.

Sometimes, though, we got lucky. Once in a while a farmer would turn out to be amenable to getting some help plowing up a new field. My father would assure him that he had done lots of plowing as a boy on a farm up north. And sure enough, his work was acknowledged with a touch of surprise, "Not too bad, young fella." Meanwhile, my mother, who in their first year of marriage had had to learn the basics of cooking from my father, struggled as best she could to help out in the kitchen, hauling water, setting the table, washing and drying dishes.

So, gradually over a month or so, sometimes sleeping in farmhouses, sometimes in our car, we reached the deep South. One day we saw two men standing by the edge of a cotton field, one tall and skinny, the other short and skinny, each with long sticks that my father told me were shotguns.

"Stop here," my mother ordered.

My father slowed down a little, but didn't stop. "I don't know about them," he said.

"I do," she replied, "I'll handle it," then leaned out the

window and called, "Would you know where we might find work?"

The two men came up to our car, one on each side, and leaned in the open windows. One poked at the steering wheel. The other patted the windshield. "My, my," he said, "ain't she a beaut?"

My father stared straight ahead; my mother shouted at him. "Go!"

Our car leaped forward and, a few seconds later, I looked out the rear window of the car and saw them laughing and then firing their shotguns into the road behind us to hasten the departure of what they very likely took to be civil rights agitators.

My parents finally did find cotton-picking work. Though they stuck with it for a couple of miserable weeks because they needed the money, they came to hate it. At the end of each day they were exhausted, aching, hot and sweaty. There was no place to wash up or cool off except the creeks, and no place to rest or sleep except in our car. I hated it too, because I was left every day sitting under a tree, far away from them, getting bitten by chiggers.

Finally, we continued south until about 50 miles from New Orleans, where we stopped for the night at the farm of people named Slager. I sat at the kitchen table eating a fresh-baked sugar cookie while Mrs. Slager and my mother chatted and laughed, stringing beans.

Three days later my parents packed up our car. I was climbing in the back when my mother reached around my waist and pulled me out. "No," she said. "You're going to stay here with Mrs. Slager until we come for you, after we get settled in a few days."

"But I want to come with you."

"For heaven's sakes," my mother hissed, annoyed and impatient with me, "you told me yourself you think Mrs. Slager is a nice lady and remember? You said you like being on this nice farm."

Mrs. Slager approached and took my hand. "Come see the baby pigs," she said.

I screamed, writhing in her grip, my feet churning, desperate to run toward my parents. But they jumped into the Buick without looking back and drove off down the road.

That night Mrs. Slager tucked me into bed. She said, "Would you like to pretend you're my little girl, just while you stay here?"

"I'm my mommy's little girl," I told her with as yet undimmed confidence, and hid under the covers until she went away.

The days went by; I followed Mrs. Slager everywhere. Together we fed the chickens and pigs, collected eggs and baked cakes. She let me drink all the milk I wanted and told me stories at bedtime. I began to call her Nanny.

Five weeks later, my father arrived to take me to our new home. "Can Nanny come too?" I asked my father. He just put me in the car without a word.

Mrs. Slager leaned through the window to give me a big kiss. Tears were pouring down her cheeks.

"I'm going to see my mommy," I told her proudly.

I never saw Mrs. Slager again.

In New Orleans, we lived in a second-floor apartment in the French Quarter, which we shared with a young man named Bert who was a friend of a friend of my mother's. What I loved best was to stand on our balcony and look down at all the people walking along the sidewalk below, smelling the spicy smells coming out of the restaurant down on the first floor. Right next to our balcony was the balcony of Bert's pal, Sonny. What Sonny loved best was to sit on his balcony with a tall drink by his side and drop pieces of ice down on the heads of people walking below. Most of them would look up, shrug and grin, though a few shook their fists when they saw us giggling. "Pay them no mind, Mighty Minerva" was Sonny's advice. Sonny called me Mighty Minerva, especially when I stamped my foot in anger. "Mighty Minerva, Mighty Minerva, Miley Merva," he teased. Sonny was my best friend.

Once a week my parents and their friends had a Prohibition party, complete with illegal hooch and shrimp from a restaurant where my father worked in the kitchen. Our apartment and Sonny's next door filled up with friends, laughter, music and chatter. I, the only child, crawled between table legs and human legs and showed off how clever I was by jumping up and down. Suddenly Sonny was there, swooping me up in his arms. "Mighty Minerva!" he shouted. "What you doin' here? You're on the wrong side of the party. You b'long my side." So we went out to our balcony and Sonny, holding me tight, started to crawl over the railing of our balcony, hovering over the street below, to the railing of his own balcony.

"Oooh, Sonny," I squealed.

"Have no fear, lil sweetheart," Sonny said, "all you got to 'member, sugar, is . . . never ever look down. That's the goddamn secret of everything, sweetness, don'cha know. Ya just look ahead, not down."

Suddenly my father was there. "What the hell do you

think you're doing?" he shouted and reached to grab me.

"Oh, sorry, old man," said Sonny, backing up and handing me over, "seemed like a good idea at the time." He swung himself over to his balcony, turned and said, "It's safe to hand her over now, y'know."

"You're drunk and you're crazy," said my father.

"Yeah," said Sonny, "and whatever else you're thinking about me. But don't you forget one thing. Me and your kid . . . well, I love this little button. Which is more than you . . . "

But my father had turned his back. He carried me off the balcony, set me down, and pushed me into the living room. "Don't you have anything more to do with him, hear me?" Then he went back to the party.

I stood motionless for a minute, then got down on my hands and knees and crawled behind the big red chair that sat near the balcony. I peeked out to see if I could glimpse Sonny on his balcony. And there he was, peeking at me! For the next few minutes we played the game of hide-and-peek until our housemate Bert, who had been standing on the balcony enjoying the view, turned, saw me, saw Sonny, and said, "Hey, what's up?"

"Game of catch," said Sonny. "Toss 'er here."

"Right," said Bert, who promptly picked me up and chucked me over the railings to Sonny. I felt myself flying, flying through the air and I screamed with laughter, even though my stomach felt hollow-funny. Sonny caught me, staggered back and sat down hard with me still in his arms.

"Gotcha, Merva, old gal," he said. "You 'n' me, we make a good pair, lil honey." Then he stood up, lifted me in his arms, called, "Here she blows!" and tossed me back to Bert.

Bert was ready. And so was Sonny the next time Bert threw me. And back and forth I flew 'til a crowd gathered on both balconies, the men laughing; "Lord, there goes Sonny, up to his old tricks," and the women gasping and shrieking, "Oh, Sonny, for God's sakes, be careful with her."

"Sonny, quit it. Bert, hand her over," said my mother, who had come out to see what the commotion was about. She snatched me up, took me into the bedroom and put me on the bed. "No more," she said, and left, locking the door behind.

I lay there on the bed, singing a little song to myself, "Sonny, honey, honey, Sonny," until I fell asleep.

Later, after the party was over, I woke to hear my parents quarreling.

"You are so sleeping with him," said my father. "What the hell has he got that you think you want? He's nothing but a drunk."

My mother's voice was hard. "You wouldn't have a clue," she replied.

A week later we left New Orleans and headed back to New York City.

Whether my father had found The Heart of America during those months, I doubt. I do know that my mother had begun her long gypsy journey through men.

Zayde and Bubbe

My paternal grandparents, Samuel and Sarah Gitlin, came from a small Russian town near the Polish border. They had an arranged marriage: Samuel, an 18-year-old blacksmith; Sarah, considered an old maid at 23, though why she was an old maid is a mystery to me. She was a hard worker and pictures show that she was a handsome young woman, even beautiful, with high cheekbones, a turned-up nose and sweet lips. She was very short, no more than 4'10" (a height I inherited more than 50 years later) with a solid body (that I didn't inherit). She was also exceptionally strong, not only in body but in will. Perhaps it was this latter quality that scared off possible suitors.

The two of them came to America when my grandfather was about to be forced into the Russian army, no place for a Jew.

They arrived in 1896 by third class on a freighter run by both steam and sails. It took them five weeks to reach Ellis Island. The crossing was terrible, with scores of courageous, desperate immigrants packed in under dreadful circumstances. Many old people and babies died of starvation and disease. Samuel, Sarah and their two children, my Aunt Ida and Uncle Max, almost met the same fate.

Once they settled in New York City, though, my grandfather was lucky and got a job in the garment industry where he made good money, always respected for his trustworthiness and excellent work. Many other Jewish immigrants weren't as fortunate – a great-uncle of mine found only the most menial of jobs, hauling heavy loads of coal up flight after flight of stairs to people's apartments, six days a week, week after week.

After three years, Samuel got word that several of his landsmen – people from his Russian village – had been settled on farms in Colchester, Connecticut, helped by the great Jewish philanthropist, Baron de Hirsch. My grandfather was able to borrow some money and with it, plus his savings, bought a good farm in Colchester. He and my grandmother remained farmers for the rest of their lives.

My father, the fourth of their six children, the child

who was the best at his school lessons, who loved to hide away from his family to read books, was the child who had to work the hardest on the farm. Books don't keep a farm running. My father was thought useful instead as the physically strongest and most competent child in the family and, so he was the hardest-worked by my grandfather, a niche my father resented all his life.

The first farm my grandparents owned overlooked a beautiful valley, had fairly fertile soil and a handsome, well-built house. Their last four children were born there – my Aunt Mary, my father (originally Meyer, but changed to Murray when he became an adult), my Uncle Bernie and, last, my Aunt Beatrice (known as Beatie or Bea). When all except Beatie had grown and left home, my grandparents sold their farm and bought a smaller one. It had only 10 acres, a huge, ugly house with six bedrooms, a small barn and a woodshed. This is the farm I remember from my childhood.

My grandparents worked very hard all of their lives. They always carried a second mortgage on their farms. Nevertheless, they were highly respected by their neighbors.

I was four years old – some months after our road trip to New Orleans – when I was taken to live for a while with my grandparents. Their existence was a complete surprise to me. I had never seen or heard of a Zayde or Bubbe until the day my mother packed a small suitcase with my clothes and announced that my daddy would take me up to Colchester to live with them for a while. She said I would like living there because they had cows and chickens and horses. Like Mrs. Slager's farm the year before! That sounded pretty good to me.

"Will you and Daddy live there too?" I wanted to know.

"No, not for now," she said.

Since my father "despised" (his word) his parents, particularly his mother, whom he called a "cow," he avoided visiting them whenever possible. Perhaps he was simply ashamed of them. His parents spoke English poorly – indeed, my grandmother hardly spoke it at all. Yiddish was her language all her life. Though my grandfather could read English and carefully went through the local newspaper every day, my grandmother was completely illiterate. As the first person in his family ever to attend a university, my father was probably mortified by his origins. Certainly Zayde and Bubbe were not people my father could ever introduce to my mother's sophisticated, worldly parents, who lived in a beautiful apartment on the Upper West Side of New York, with a view of Central Park.

My father and I drove to Colchester in a borrowed car. (My parents had had to sell the beautiful Buick that my grandfather had given them the year before.) Once there, my father jumped out, grabbed my suitcase and set me on the ground. As he walked me over to the barn, my grandfather appeared at the door – a smiling man with a gentle demeanor, a walrus mustache and ruddy skin.

"This is Joyce, Pa," my father said. And before my grandfather could reply, my father said, "Well," then turned and strode quickly back to the car. And sped away.

At that moment, my grandmother opened the kitchen door and, taking in the scene, shook her head, pointed to the disappearing car and agitatedly spoke some words to her husband in a strange language. Zayde shrugged, gently took my hand and walked me over to Bubbe who never, for a moment, stopped talking. Immediately she caught me up and gave me a great squeeze that took my breath away. She was solid and soft at the same time, smelling of soap, farmer's cheese and fresh-baked bread.

Zayde next took me out to a field where six cows were grazing. "Boss! Here, Boss!" he hollered and then, wonder of wonders, they all stopped, lifted their heads and began to plod toward us. My heart thumped and I held Zayde's hand tightly, but those huge animals moved with such stately, shambling awkwardness that I began to giggle. They looked a little like giant marionettes.

Zayde looked down with a smile and lifted me up in his arms. "Little Joycela, sweet little one, we will make you happy here." It was evening milking time by then, and as each cow entered the barn she seemed to know which stall was hers, except for one of the smallest who started to back up until Zayde gave her a smack on her behind. Then she went straight to her stall as though she and Zayde had come to some sort of understanding.

Oh, at first they were scary, those cows, too big and sometimes too close to me. But I also loved them right from the start, their huge, warm bodies, all with their funny-looking, nippley bags hanging underneath, their fly-swishing tails, their big liquid eyes, their wide, wet noses and mouths, the rich smell of their piss and plops – everything about them, especially with my Zayde close by, seemed both exciting and, after a little while, safe. As I watched Zayde pull their teats and heard the *zsss, zsss* of the milk as it hit the metal pail, I entered a new world where all my senses came bursting alive at once, especially smell and touch. My Zayde smelled as rich and wonderful as those cows he was milking did. He smelled of cows, of hay, of manure and of sweat and pipe tobacco. For all the time I lived with him, I would creep close to him to breathe him in and feel his heat, his sweetness, his rough gentleness.

Every morning and every evening I would follow Zayde to the barn to "help" him milk the cows. I'd bring him the empty pails or wave the flies from his head. The first time he gave me a dipperful of milk to drink I made a face. "It tastes bad," I told him.

"It tastes of cow," said Zayde. "Is good when you get used to it." And he was right.

Once in a while, Zayde would tell me to open my mouth, bend down near a cow's udder and he'd squirt a little milk into my mouth. I would jump up and down with delight. Sometimes a little of the milk would drip down the front of my clean dress. *Oy.* When Zayde and I would go into the house for breakfast, a little bit in fear of what Bubbe might say, Bubbe would just look at me, then at Zayde, shake her head and give me a little shove, saying "neh, neh, neh." But we knew she wasn't really angry because she would then lean down and put her warm hand on my head in a way that made me feel safe, after, of course, she first shook a finger at Zayde.

Twice a week, after the morning milking, Zayde would hitch up the two horses, Prince and Chubb, load the wagon with tall, full milk cans, and deliver his milk to the train station where, when the train came in, his full cans would be put into one of the freight cars to be taken to the milk company's processing plant, and his empties returned. Sometimes Zayde would take me with him and would sit me on his lap and let me hold the reins. He showed me how to pull the correct rein while yelling "Gee!" when he wanted the horses to turn right and "Haw!" for left. I sat perched up there feeling like a grownup, looking down on the world from the safety of Zayde's warm lap, feeling the sway of the wagon as the horses patiently clopped, clopped their way to town. At the station Zayde and Mr. Ross, the stationmaster, would unload the milk cans and say a few words to each other. Mr. Ross always checked the cans that the other farmers brought to the station, but he never checked Zayde's milk cans. He knew that Zayde never, ever shorted the milk company.

Mr. Ross was not the only person in Colchester who trusted my grandfather. The two dozen or so Jewish men in the town, not generally men who trusted anyone, had learned that, if important papers had to be kept safe, it was Samuel Gitlin who they should ask to hold onto them. If a secret had to be kept, only Samuel should share it. If a decision had to be made, go to Samuel for the wisest advice. If a quarrel was getting out of hand, let Samuel Gitlin be the Solomon who would end it. Sometimes it was hard to pinpoint what he had done to solve a problem because what he had done seemed so innocuous.

I remember one evening going with my grandfather to a meeting of the Colchester Jewish men to discuss whether they had enough families to start a synagogue in town, when suddenly a quarrel broke out between two of them, Mr. Shmulsky and Mr. Feigleman. Mr. Feigleman had made the mistake of reminding Mr. Shmulsky that Shmulsky owed him $36.45.

"Me? I owe you nothing!" Shmulsky haughtily replied.

"*Vat?*" roared Feigleman, enraged. "You, you . . . *gonif!* You dare to say you owe me nothing? *Oy gevalt,* what kind of crook I lent my money to?"

And in short order the whole room seemed to be full of shouting men on one side or the other of the argument.

My grandfather rose from his chair, which in itself quieted some of the men. He went over to Mr. Feigleman and laid his hand gently on the man's arm. "Listen to dat thief, Sam," Mr. Feigleman said. "You know the truth! You was there when Shmulsky and me agreed, right? That *gonif* owes me $36.45, right?"

"Of course, Sid, we all know Jake owes you $36.45," my grandfather said quietly. "Aha!" Mr. Feigleman beamed at the other men in victory.

"But, Sid, do you know what date he pays you the money?" asked my grandfather gently.

"Sure, I know, oh boy, I know," Mr. Feigleman replied and winked at everyone, smiling broadly. "By February 7th it is."

"Aha!" Mr. Shmulsky broke in. "So what I tell you? In February I'm owing him $36.45. But in October . . . right now, yes? . . . I'm owing him nothing!!"

And, one by one, the men in the room nodded and set the quarrel aside.

"So, good friends, let us now move on to our main consideration," my Zayde said.

And with that, Mr. Feigleman, looking a bit stunned, softly said, "Oh vell," and the discussion returned to should or should not the synagogue be built. This was something Feigleman and Shmulsky could agree on.

My Bubbe was perhaps the only person who didn't seem to find my Zayde to be one of the finest men to walk the earth. I think in her heart she knew he was an exceptionally good man but, according to her lights, he didn't work hard enough or long enough or well enough. She was a holy terror, that Bubbe of mine.

Nothing remained the same once she got her hands on it. She worked early and she worked late, never stopping except to eat a little food and sleep a few hours. Her hands and arms were enormously strong from hauling sacks of flour and grain and pails of water, kneading bread, preparing huge pots of soup, churning butter and scrubbing clothes on a washboard, making beds, mopping floors and feeding the chickens.

To earn extra money, Bubbe and Zayde took in boarders during the summer. These summer boarders usually consisted of one or more families from New York or Boston, looking to get relief from the oppressive city heat by spending time in the country, eating good healthy kosher food and breathing fresh air. The wives and children would often stay for a month or more. The husbands, who only had short vacations from their jobs, were usually unable to stay for more than a week, sometimes driving up to my grandparents' farm on weekends for the rest of the summer.

During the months I lived with Zayde and Bubbe, a new family, the Rosenbaums, came as summer guests. They planned to stay for a month. There were Mr. and Mrs. Rosenbaum (Mr. R. only on weekends) and the two boys, ages 8 and 10. The boys spent almost all their time outdoors. And then there was Mrs. Rosenbaum's old father, Mr. Kaminsky, a runt of a man with false teeth that clacked a lot and that he would often remove.

One day after breakfast, Bubbe gave me something to carry into the pantry and put on a shelf. When I turned to leave the pantry, there was Mr. Kaminsky, smiling at me with his yellow false teeth. His breath smelled bad. "Ah, ah, what a pretty little girl she is in her pretty little pink dress." He beamed, leaning over me and poking me on the chest with his bony fingers.

"Yes," I said proudly, "my Aunt Beatie sewed the roses."

"Did she, hah? My, my, my, what a smart lady is your Auntie Beatie," he said. He stepped closer to inspect the roses on my chest. His breath smelled awful. "And did that vunderful Auntie Beatie put little pink roses on your little pink bloomers to match?"

"Oh, no," I said witheringly, "that's silly. Aunt Beatie wouldn't put roses on my bloomers."

"So," said Mr. Kaminsky, as he pulled my panties down a bit, "no little pink roses even here?" and he pointed to my belly button. "Not even here?" asked Mr. Kaminsky as his fingers moved farther down.

Then suddenly Mr. Kaminsky seemed to fly backward out of the pantry and I saw my Bubbe push him up against the pantry door. "Dirty, dirty, bad!" Bubbe yelled in her broken English. "You don't go near baby girl, you *alter kocker*." I didn't understand. Was Bubbe mad at Mr. Kaminsky just because he smelled bad?

Mrs. Rosenbaum came running and when she saw me with my dress pulled up and her father there with his face twisted, her face turned red. "Papa, no," she said and began to cry. "Please, please," she said to Bubbe. "He's just an old man."

"Old, young, he got to know better," said Bubbe. "You take him away, missus. He not stay here no more," she declared firmly.

Two days later, on Saturday morning, Mr. Rosenbaum drove up from New York and picked up his family. Zayde stayed in the barn while it was happening but Bubbe stood at the kitchen door with one hand on her hip and the other firmly on my head as the Rosenbaums trooped out. "You nice people but you keep that one away from little girls," she said as they left, pointing to Mr. Kaminsky, whose eyes were cast down inspecting the kitchen linoleum.

Then, as the Rosenbaums' car left our yard, Bubbe turned to me and said, "So, nuh, now is time you get corn and give to chickens. I go make cheese." And she gave my head a little thump to remind me to do it properly.

A few months after I began living with Zayde and Bubbe, all my aunts, uncles and cousins came for a big party, a Seder. The women bustled around the kitchen and talked, talked, talked. The men put tables together and brought chairs from all over the house and bantered and teased each other. They set up a huge table, three tables put together, covered with huge white sheets.

Once the dinner began, I was allowed to sit on my Zayde's lap – though my Aunt Ida would periodically remove me because she thought Zayde was spoiling me. We ate, then stopped eating and did funny things on the tablecloth with salt. We chanted for a while, then ate some more and did more strange stuff. I slipped off Zayde's lap and ran and ran, round and round and round the table.

"What's the matter with that child?" my Aunt Mary asked.

"Oh, my dear, she's just happy," Zayde said.

So my life continued with Zayde and Bubbe, late spring, summer and fall of 1929. I always spent some of my day watching Bubbe work, helping her make beds, fetching plates and food she needed from the pantry. She knew just what she was doing and how to do it. But it was Zayde whom I loved deeply and with whom I spent as much of my time as possible, following him around the farm, always staying close to him.

One day, Zayde and I were in the barn. He was shoveling some grain for the cows and I was bringing him a bigger scoop. Zayde looked up and quietly said, "You know, Joycela, my little darling, your mama and papa are coming to take you home. Tomorrow morning."

I stared at Zayde. His face looked sad. My breath felt tight. "But I want to live with you and Bubbe. I don't want to go with them," I said.

"Yes, I wish you could stay here, sweetheart," Zayde said, "but you belong with Mama and Papa."

"No, no, Zayde," I cried, "please, I don't want to go away. I'll be gooder, Zayde, and I'll help you more. I'll help you lots and lots, Zayde. See, see?" I began to drag a heavy bucket of grain to him. "See? You need me!"

Zayde came over to me and put his arms around me and we stood that way, gently rocking, for a long time. "Time to feed the chickens," he finally said, wiping his eyes, and picked up a scoop of corn. I shook my head when he tried to hand it to me, so he carried it in one hand and held my hand with the other and he fed the chickens for me. That evening I wouldn't eat supper and Bubbe gave me a little pat on the cheek and said, "You not eat, you get sick," but that didn't work.

That night I lay in bed, thinking hard. After a while I heard Zayde and Bubbe go to bed. Looking for a hiding place, I got up, crawled under the bed and fell asleep. Then, in the middle of the night, I woke up. Under the bed wasn't good enough. I crept downstairs and hid behind a big can of flour that Bubbe had put in the pantry. I had to push the can a little so there was enough space for me to hide. It was scary in there, so dark, but I thought they would never think to look for me there until it was too late and my mommy and daddy had left. After a while I fell asleep.

Next morning, I heard Bubbe and Zayde when they came downstairs. Soon I heard Bubbe go back upstairs to see where I was. She came down again and I heard her call Zayde to see if I was in the barn. I could hear them calling and calling.

It took them about 15 more minutes to find me in the pantry. *"Oy, oy, oy,"* said Bubbe, shaking her head, then she gave me a big kiss on the cheek, which she had never done before. Zayde took me into the kitchen, set me on his knee, wrapped his arms around me and told me a little story about how the village of Cholmodsky beat the devil. I hid my face in his chest the whole time.

I finally agreed to get dressed. Bubbe packed my bag and, later that morning, my parents drove into the yard. Bubbe marched out to their car and tried to persuade my parents to come in and have some of her fresh coffeecake and milk but they shook their heads. Seeming uncertain for what may have been one of the first times in her life, she stood for a moment, then suddenly wheeled around and grabbed me and kissed me hard on both cheeks. Zayde took my hand and my suitcase and we walked toward the car.

My father got out and nodded to Zayde. "Hello, Pop," he said, unsmiling. My mother got out of the car as well. She walked over to Zayde and, in her high, light voice said, "Thank you for keeping her." Then she turned to me and said, "Well, you certainly have grown, Joyce. So now it's time for us to leave."

I clung to Zayde who kept patting me and murmuring, "You good girl. You my little sweetheart."

Finally he lifted me up and tried to get me to look at him but I wouldn't. He carried me over to the car and set me down on the back seat. "You come soon to visit; you come lots to visit," he said. But I didn't believe him and I wouldn't look at him. He closed the door and my parents got in the car and we drove off.

There was an old brown plaid blanket on the back seat that smelled of mildew. I crawled under it and stayed there all the way back to New York City.

Journey to Albania

They fought a lot. Usually it was because my father wouldn't get a job and my mother had to support him.

"But I already have a job," said my father. "Writing a novel is my job."

"Yeah? Well, you could sit in that armchair from now 'til doomsday," replied my mother, "writing, writing, writing that boring novel of yours, and you still couldn't make it good enough."

"Oh, I know just what you're really saying," spat my father. "You mean I'll never achieve the perfect writing of Mr. Perfection, your perfect daddy."

I sat very still in my chair and pretended to be reading, reading, reading my book. Other fights were about me, and I didn't understand why.

"All you do with Joyce is pretend she's not here," said my mother.

"Well, I don't see you giving her much of your time," said my father.

"This was a big mistake," she said.

As their fight escalated, I scurried to the dark, safer place between the back of the couch and the radiator. I knew what they were saying.

I was now five years old. After my time at Bubbe and Zayde's farm, my parents and I had stayed at my other grandparents' summer home in Sheffield, Massachusetts in the Berkshires. One of our neighbors, Mrs. Carey, was the sweet teacher of the one-room schoolhouse just a half-mile up our road and she told my parents she would like to teach me because she thought I was "a smart little pumpkin" and could do at least first-grade work. So I went for a couple of months where I was the youngest child in the place. I loved it. Mrs. Carey showed me where I would sit. She introduced me to my fellow students, ages 7 to 15. But she forgot to tell me one important thing – where the outhouse was. And for some reason I was shy about asking. It was about six weeks after I'd started school; I was up at the blackboard working on arithmetic sums; I peed so much so that it puddled on the floor. I filled with shame and ran outside.

Mrs. Carey came outside and tried to tell me not to be embarrassed and to come back in. But I would not. I waited outside for my daddy to come for me and I told him I was never going back to Mrs. Carey's school.

"Well, maybe you could take a day or two off," my father said.

"No," I said. "I won't go." And I never did.

Mrs. Carey brought me schoolbooks to read and papers with sums for me to work out and I did some schoolwork at home. "She's too bright not to be in school," Mrs. Carey said. But no one could persuade me.

Two months later, we moved to a tiny fourth-floor walkup in Brooklyn. On and off, my parents would discuss what to do with me. My father was absolutely opposed to my returning to Bubbe and Zayde, or living with any of the family on his side, Aunt Ida, Uncle Max, Aunt Mary, Uncle Bernie or Aunt Beatie. According to him, they were all "dumb animals."

With my father's side out, the remaining option was to shuffle me off to someone on my mother's side. Until recently, my mother's parents had been living in an elegant apartment overlooking Central Park. Perhaps I could have gone there, though my mother and grandmother hated each other. I had heard my mother say she wasn't going to have her mother "lord it over her" – apparently, dropping me off to stay with them would confirm the big mistake she'd made in marrying my father. On the other hand, my mother admired my grandpa more than anyone in the world. He was a famous foreign correspondent and a newspaper publisher; he knew kings and presidents. His name was Herman Bernstein.

Six months earlier, President Hoover had appointed Herman Bernstein to be the American ambassador to Albania, a position officially known as the Envoy Extraordinary and Minister Plenipotentiary. My grandparents, Herman and Sophie, and my mother's younger sisters, Dorothy and Violet, had all gone to live in Tirana, Albania's capital.

One day my father received a letter from my ambassador grandfather containing an ultimatum: Get a job or I'll see to it that my daughter divorces you. My father was so angry, he didn't speak to my mother or me for a whole week. Then he gave in. He took the "goddamn job" my grandpa had found for him as Assistant Director of a big community center on Chicago's West Side – the Jewish People's Institute. In three weeks' time, he and my mother would move to Chicago.

Perhaps unsurprisingly, I would not go with them. Instead, I would be sent me to live with my grandparents in Albania. I liked my grandparents, my grandfather especially, so I looked forward to seeing them.

A few weeks later, my mother took me down to the docks. As we threaded through hundreds of people milling around a giant ocean liner, my mother took my hand; we climbed the gangplank and made our way to the captain of the ship.

"Grandpa has arranged for Captain Morris to be in charge of you on your trip across the ocean," my mother explained.

Captain Morris, resplendent in his white cap with gold braid and his crisp uniform, leaned down to smile at me. "So, you're the brave little miss who is crossing the Atlantic alone!"

Alone? Didn't my mother say Captain Morris would be taking care of me? Dozens of people swirled around us, talking, laughing, crying, kissing, waving goodbye to the people on shore. My mother tapped my shoulder and said, "Stop looking so scared, for heaven's sakes. It's a big adventure, silly. Just be a good girl and do what the captain tells you to do and you'll be just fine. OK? Well, goodbye, Joyce. I have to go now." Then she turned away and walked down the gangplank. She didn't turn back to wave; she just disappeared.

Indeed, the captain did not become my onboard buddy. He quickly turned me over to the care of a steward and a maid, who took me to a stateroom and unpacked my clothes. The rest of that day, I clung to them, but very quickly I stopped being scared because there were so many exciting things I kept encountering.

The first morning I went down to the gigantic, formal dining room for breakfast. Two waiters bowed to me and then asked me what I would like to eat.

"Chicken and ice cream," I told them.

"Are you sure?" one of them asked. "Maybe that'd be better for lunch. Or dinner."

"I want some now," I replied.

And, oh, what nice men they were! They brought me orange juice, toast, a nicely roasted chicken breast and, yes, my favorite vanilla ice cream.

By the second day, I had begun to feel like a character from one of my favorite books, *The Elephant's Child,* filled with "satiable curiosity" about everything and everybody around me: The rolling ship. The giant waves. The funny little round windows. The wide decks with grownups, half-sitting, half-lying, like peas in a pod, in their long deck chairs. The huge lifeboats hanging off the railings. The vast dining room with its snow-white tablecloths and sparkling crystal glassware. The huge boat stacks that sometimes honked loudly. I ran from one interesting object and person to the next, the steward faithfully following close behind to protect me.

Soon, a number of my shipmates were curious about me as well, this tiny motherless girl, who every morning skipped along the decks, always trailed by the steward. A little old lady who looked like a witch stopped me and taught me to play Slapjack with her, declaring me "a cute little smartypants" when I beat her almost every time. A teasing young man lifted me up on his shoulders and jiggedy danced with me, then played hide-and-seek with me among the lifeboats. Every day, a kewpie doll of an old lady with great round rouge spots on her cheeks brought me pretty bracelets, necklaces and pins from her jewelry box, and bonbons from her hoard of chocolates. A tall, skinny colonel saluted me and taught me to salute back; then we marched up and down the deck, me swinging my arms importantly, he playing an imaginary bugle. A lady in men's trousers wrapped me round and round in her deckchair's blanket and bet me a penny I couldn't squirm out before she finished reciting Mr. Shakespeare's poem, "Hark, Hark, the Lark!" Of course, I won the penny.

At dinner at the captain's table, I was placed beside a large lady opera singer with funny feathers in her headband who told me she had two little girls of her own and she missed them very much. When I asked for her help in cutting up my roast beef, she leaned way over me as she cut my meat, enveloping me in her ample flesh, then asked in her booming, laughing voice, "Hah, is my great big boozalom about to smother you, leettle one?"

Another night I was taken to a huge room with a dance band and put up on a table to dance. Before I knew it, a handsome man lifted me into his arms and began to twirl me round and round. Another and another laughing man whirled me until I began to feel dizzy. Beautiful women in short shiny dresses – this was the height of the Jazz Age and they were decked out in the sexiest flapper styles – gave me sips of their champagne. And at last, when midnight arrived and I was almost asleep, several of them carried me off to my stateroom. The giggling young women would choose one of the young men to undress me and put me in my pajamas and, after their derisive laughter at his awkwardness, clap and kiss his cheek for his "good" work, then tuck me into bed, leaning over to kiss me goodnight, smelling of mysterious scents: pomade, perfume and cigarettes. "Night, night!" they would call to me, as they all laughingly ran out to dance, drink and flirt their night away.

The next morning my friend, the waiter in the big dining room, noticed that I wasn't eating much of my breakfast and asked me if I had a hangover. "I think maybe I do," I told him. Even my chicken and ice cream did not taste all that good.

But finally the big ship docked at Cherbourg, all the people who had been on board disappeared and now I was riding in a train headed for Paris. Seated with me in my compartment was Mr. Krasnicki, my grandpa's aide. Short, slender and dark-haired, he had come to accompany me on the next leg of my journey. But Mr. Krasnicki had much work to do, so he paid little attention to me, busy instead writing and shuffling papers. I sat and sat, read my book over and over, stared out the window and was bored, bored, bored. The swaying train car made me feel sick and I suddenly vomited all over Mr. Krasnicki's knee. Alarmed at my white face, he climbed up on the seat, pants leg dripping, and pulled the emergency cord. In a minute, the train screeched to a halt. I curled up into a ball as agitated grownup voices bounced back and forth over my head.

The train started up again but, in a few minutes, gradually slowed and stopped. Loud French voices argued back and forth, then a heavy man picked me up and took me outside. Waiting there was a nun. Beside her was a stretcher, onto which I was put to be carried off to what looked like a castle but was in fact a Catholic hospital. "I want my grandpa!" I yelled as they carted me away.

"Mon dieu," moaned Mr. Krasnicki, who must have been terrified to report this turn of events to his employer.

The hospital was beautiful, with a large marble entrance hall which overlooked a delightful garden filled with an amazing variety of flowers. On each side of the front hall were doors to the patients' rooms.

Things did not begin well between the nuns and me. I was taken by two young nuns to a large room filled with cribs, all but two empty, and put into one of them. Enraged, I immediately protested. "I am not a baby! I will not sleep in a stupid crib!" When I started to climb out of it, the nuns set me back in – only to have me climb out again. Then the Mother Superior, a woman of about 50, tall and firm, picked me up, put me in the crib and said gently, "It is not so bad. It is only for sleeping at night and maybe a little nap in the afternoon, yes? And we will also keep one railing down so you can climb down. But you must promise not to climb down at night. Call us if you need to go to the bathroom. But you must sleep there always at night."

Then she took my hand and helped me out of the crib, washed me and changed my clothes and, best of all, introduced me to everyone: the other nuns, the gardeners, the cooks and even the other patients, most of whom were very old. Almost all of them smiled at me. That Mother Superior lived up to her title; she was brilliant at dealing with obstreperous little girls. And I had discovered an important fact of life: nuns always win.

It was decided that I would stay for one week, not because I was actually ill but because my grandfather and Mr. Krasnicki required it to assuage their concerns. It turned out to be, like the ocean crossing, one of the more beautiful weeks of my childhood. I was given free rein to pick flowers from the garden, though the gardening nun and chief gardener first pointed out which special flowers could not be picked. By the third day, however, I was picking a few of those illegal flowers and no one stopped me. Once I had picked a good bunch, I would carry my bouquet indoors, knock at a patient's door, holler *"Allo!"* to wake them up if they were asleep, sing *"Frère Jacques"* twice over in my best French accent, and place my bouquet on the patient's chest. Not a single one of those patients ever complained about me and several sang along with me in their reedy voices. One of the young nuns told me I was helping the patients get well faster.

"Can I be a nun?" I asked her.

"Not for a while," she said with a smile.

I loved those gentle, tough women and that beautiful hospital. I could have stayed there for many more days. But after the week was up, my Aunt Violet came for me. She was my mother's younger sister, the one who was pretty and charming, especially with men. She and I took the train to Paris. When we got off the train, a dozen newspapermen and cameramen crowded around us to interview me, this tiny girl who had crossed the Atlantic alone. Flashbulbs exploded as they shot pictures and questions at me, but when one reporter asked if I was for or against the Gold Standard, Aunt Violet snorted haughtily and told him, "Don't be ridiculous," whisking me into a cab and off to the hotel to meet her sister Dorothy and continue our journey to Albania.

After its dark beginning behind my parents' couch, the year I was five would become perhaps the happiest year of my childhood. I would learn that year what it meant to feel both secure and free. And I fell head over heels in love.

At that time Tirana, Albania's capital, was nothing but a large village, mostly filled with little stone and mudbrick huts, their peasant owners living in the same dwellings as their geese, donkeys, and goats. Big old bullock carts, donkeys and horses clopped up and down the cobblestone streets. In the center of Tirana, there was a large, lively marketplace, bursting with colorful fruits and vegetables, chickens and geese squawking in crates. In other stalls, women were painting red, white and blue wooden toys.

Two landmarks stood out starkly from the rest of Tirana. First, looming over Tirana was King Zog's dark, gloomy, silent palace, built of a rough, brownish-gray granite with windows covered with bars like a prison, though handsomely curved instead of straight. The other landmark was Albania's only four-lane highway, spectacularly straight, wide and well-built, running from the Adriatic seacoast and ending at the palace. It had been built by Mussolini's engineers and was Mussolini's clever way of making sure that Italy partially owned Albania. Likely King Zog had no clue of Mussolini's designs. For him, the thoroughfare provided him and his many sisters a grand way to show off his spacious, elegant, open touring car, which they all rode in on the weekends as he waved majestically to his subjects.

The American embassy was much nicer than the palace. It consisted of three attractive white wooden buildings: my grandfather's offices on the left, the guards' house on the right and the large, graceful embassy house in the center. To enter the embassy complex, one had hardly to wait more than a few seconds for a guard to come running and open the heavy, handsomely scrolled iron gates, saluting and clicking his heels, then waving us on. From the start, I was enchanted by the handsome guards; one of them was to become perhaps the most important (and painful) love object of my childhood.

My grandmother, Sophie, was as refined and beautiful as a duchess. She was in charge of the indoor and garden servants, about 10 in all, and was extremely skilled at making sure each of them did their duty. To me, the most amazing of these servants were the Hungarian chef and his kitchen helpers. They seemed to inhabit a mysterious and frantically friendly underworld down in the basement. At dinnertime, the chef would place his delicious dishes onto a small hand-operated dumbwaiter, ringing a bell to notify the butler. The butler would pull the ropes, open the paneled door and, voilà, the dishes would magically appear, whereupon they were solemnly carried over to our dining room table and served to my grandmother. She would take a tiny taste, then nod her head, after which we would all get served: Grandpa first of course, me last.

I would sometimes sneak down into the basement kitchen where the chefs fed me bits of their goodies. When they discovered it was the dumbwaiter that fascinated me the most and that I wanted to take a ride in it, the chefs told me, "No, no, not good. Madame" – meaning my grandma – "never let you play there."

This only meant to me that someday I would find a way to do it on my own.

Besides these kitchen servants, there was a British personal maid for my grandmother and a French one for my two aunts, plus several Albanian cleaners. For some reason, I was rewarded with the hard-nosed Frau Kochbein, a German nurse who tried her damnedest to regulate my meals, my bedtime and my bowels. The more she tried the more I resisted. My grandmother attempted a concord between us, talking to each of us separately in hopes that we would agree to at least try to get along with each other. It wasn't easy. My nurse spoke very little English; I spoke no German.

One day, for some reason, we decided to make a tiny effort to understand each other better. We managed somehow to convince each other that we understood the meaning of at least one word: schleppus. I thought I had at last discovered the German word for slippers. At the same time, Frau Kochbein was convinced she had unearthed the English word for slippers. In triumph, we went to my grandma and announced, with all sincerity, that "schleppus" meant the same in both languages! My grandma laughed her tinkly laugh and we walked off feeling a little better about each other. Not for long, though, and soon we were fighting again. My grandmother finally found another place for Frau Kochbein at another ministry, and after that I was basically on my own.

That suited me just fine. Sometimes, especially when there was a full or nearly-full moon at night, I would wake up, get out of bed and wander around the house. One night I decided I would at last take a ride on the dumbwaiter. I opened its little folding door, hauled the dumbwaiter up from the kitchen, and squeezed myself onto the platform, inadvertently hitting the folding door which then slammed shut. I was left in a tiny, pitch black space, unable to figure out how to open the door. I pulled on the rope. It needed more muscle than I had to move it. I pushed and pulled on the door but nothing happened. I began to cry. No one came. I wailed.

Sometime later, I heard voices calling me. "Joyce, Joyce, where are you?"

"Here! Let me out!" I cried.

"Where on earth do you suppose she has gone to?" I heard my grandmother say.

"Here, here, here," I shouted and banged on the dumbwaiter door.

"That banging sounds like it's out in the garden," my Aunt Violet said.

"No, no, I'm in the dumbwaiter!" I yelled.

"Now that you mention it I do hear something," said my grandmother.

"Grandma, Grandma, it's me," I screamed.

"Mama, I think we've scared her long enough," I heard my sweet Aunt Dorothy say. And with that she opened the dumbwaiter door and pulled me up and out.

Next morning, when I visited Aunt Dorothy's bedroom, I said to her, "Do you know why they call it a dumbwaiter? 'Cause it's a dumb, dumb thing that some dummy invented." She gave me a hug and a squirt of her French perfume.

My aunts often allowed me to visit them in their bedroom, where they rose late every morning, and might let me to stroke their silken nightgowns and fluffy powder puffs. Sometimes their French maid would weave flowers into my braids.

One of my favorite parts of each day was the visit I was allowed to make to my roly-poly but very dignified grandpa, dressed formally in a three-piece suit and stiff collar, at his desk in the embassy office. He would put me on his lap and let me write words with his fancy pen and then blot them with his fancy blotter. Then he would pull out his big gold pocket watch, held by a long gold chain, and let me listen to its loud tick. He was not a good storyteller like my other grandfather, Zayde, but his closest friend, the German ambassador, was a wonderful one.

Once a week, Grandpa and I would go to the German embassy to visit him. That dear man loved to re-tell fairy tales and, though I had already read many fairy tales, he told ones that I had never ever heard of. Some had scary animals in them, but I was never scared when I was with him. I remember what a kind, gentle man he was, how much I loved him and how much my grandpa did too. He would sit me on his lap and, after he told me his remarkable fairytales, he would describe his dear grandchildren to me so well that I wrote little letters to them because I was sure they were my good friends.

Looking back now, I realize this deeply fine man was very

likely killed years later by the Nazis; like my grandfather, he was a Jew. I have always wondered what might have happened if my grandfather had lived longer – he died at the age of 51 in 1931, not long after my stay with him and my grandmother in Albania. Might he have saved his dear friend and brought him to America?

My very favorite place at the embassy was the guards' house where the Albanian guards and chauffeurs gathered – black-haired, black-eyed, lean and hawk-nosed men, as exciting as pirates. They were headed by a man named Kemal and one of them in particular, Kemal's nephew Rassim, was the gentlest, kindest, most patient and most trustworthy young man I had ever met. (Which, in retrospect, was truly remarkable in this tribal warrior nation.) He must have been all of 19 years old. He had an amazing ability to imitate the birdsongs of dozens of birds. His whistling was beautiful. He was beautiful. Whenever I looked at him I must have shown the world all my feelings of tenderness and happiness I felt toward him. The other men began to elbow him and tell him that I had fallen in love with him. They had gotten that right.

Almost every morning after breakfast I would run to talk with Rassim. I would tell him what my yesterday had been like, all the things I had done, and what I thought my today might be like. I would tell him about everything that mattered to me: whom I had talked with, who had said what to whom, where I was going today. He always patiently listened to me and, when I was sad, he would coax me out of my sadness by whistling some of his gorgeous birdsongs and tell me all would turn out well. He would lift me up on his shoulder and run around the circular driveway as I beat him on the head and said, "Go horsey, go!" And then he'd put me down, pat me gently on the head and laughingly wish me a good day.

"I am going to marry Rassim," I informed Aunt Dorothy.

"How lovely," she said. "Just don't tell Grandpa or Grandma yet."

One day I saw Rassim talking to one of the maids, the prettiest one, a gypsy girl named Dani. They were laughing and flirting. Burning with jealousy and fury, I ran up to Rassim and butted him with my head, crying, "I hate you, you big nothing!"

The next day I stayed indoors. The day after I walked around the garden but not to the front courtyard. On the third day, I walked down to the gate but pretended I hadn't seen Rassim. He tried some of his bird whistles but I pretended not to hear. On the fourth day, I was so lonely I walked up to him and leaned my head on his hip, searching for something important to tell him. "Yesterday I broke my dolly's head," I said sadly, though in fact it was my own small heart that was in pieces.

"Aw, too bad, little bossie," he said sympathetically. "We be good friends now, yes?"

I nodded, happy and at peace, at last.

Rassim's uncle Kemal was also the embassy's chief chauffeur. Once a week, he would drive my grandmother, my aunts Dorothy and Violet, and me around Tirana and we would stop at the marketplace to buy food, hair products, and handmade lace. At the stall with the wooden toys, I had my eye on a little blue-striped horse. What a great day it was when my grandma bought it for me.

Once in a while, she would order Kemal to take us out

into the country for "a healthful change of scene." Once, our outing took us up into the Dajti mountains, a few miles east of Tirana. We had a long, stately Buick limousine, befitting an embassy, which Kemal usually drove cautiously, as befits the driver of a vehicle of state, weaving among men, women and donkeys carrying goods to market. But on this particular day, as we rode up the mountains, Kemal began to go faster and faster, sweeping around the blind curves of the narrow, winding road, with cliffs on one side, a sheer drop on the other.

For some reason, my grandmother did not try to slow him down. Perhaps she rather liked doing something a little wild for a change. When I told her I felt sick to my stomach, she told me to hang my head out the window so I could vomit on the road, not on the upholstery. As Kemal barreled up the mountain path, we continued to pass, and barely miss, a wide array of humanity: farmers with carts carrying chickens and ducks, women wearing huge baskets of laundry or produce on their heads, lanky cows plodding slowly in spite of being constantly whipped with willow branches by children, Greek Orthodox priests astride their ragged donkeys clopping slowly down the mountain, young couples holding hands and laughing.

Finally, Kemal rounded a corner too fast and collided with a cart drawn by a donkey and filled with cackling geese. The donkey panicked and ran over the precipice. The cart would have followed if it hadn't, by a miracle, gotten hung up on a small tree. The geese flapped and squawked hysterically; the donkey hung below, kicking and braying. The peasant, whose cart and donkey it was, began wailing and wringing his hands.

"My God, Kemal, what have you done?" cried my grandmother.

"No worry, madam," he replied. "Kemal fix." Whereupon he burst out of the car and began to yell at and shove the poor peasant.

My usually restrained and seemingly fragile grandmother had had enough. She rushed out of our limousine, ordered Kemal back into the car, paid the peasant a sum equal to the cart and donkey, returned to the car and, as Kemal started up the engine, said to him, "Kemal, The American Embassy Does Not Hit People!"

Back in the car, Aunt Dorothy, the gentler of my two aunts, was close to tears over the fate of the poor little donkey; Aunt Violet just snorted and spat out a single word, "Men."

Kemal returned us to the embassy in complete silence. When we pulled into the drive, my grandmother announced, "This is the last time we will take the mountain air, thank you."

"Yes, madam," said Kemal, allowing himself the tiniest of shrugs. We could almost hear what he was thinking, "Women!"

❧

Dorothy and Violet were both of marriageable age, 21 and 19. Aunt Violet was the more outgoing and vivacious, but also quick to mock and make fun of men. Both had many suitors, including glittering Albanian cavalry men and earnest young diplomatic secretaries from other embassies. My aunts would peer out the window, hidden behind curtains, when these young men would stroll or ride their horses past our embassy in the hope of getting a glimpse of those two lovely (and, they assumed, wealthy) young American ladies.

My aunts enjoyed these spectacles immensely, Violet commenting and Dorothy giggling about how badly one rode his horse, how another was so fat he wobbled as he walked, how another had a ridiculous moustache. My grandfather kept a careful eye on his daughters, particularly Violet, who tended to be a flirt. What he didn't realize was that it was Dorothy he should have been watching because she had fallen in love with a young Hungarian medical student she had met in Geneva a few months before and whom she was determined to marry.

A few months later, my Aunt Dorothy sneaked off and eloped, then, with some trepidation, brought her new husband back to the embassy to meet my grandfather. That first evening was something of a disaster. My Uncle Nicky, tall, dark-haired and handsome, with full, cherry-red lips, sat down to his first embassy dinner. The main dish that night was squab. There was one squab for each person at the dinner – bigger ones for the men, smaller ones for the women. My grandfather was served first and took his large squab. As the guest of honor, my new Uncle Nicky was served next to also take a large squab. "Ah," he said, "magnificent little birds!" and then helped himself to two of the small ones. There was a profound silence as the butler offered the platter next to my grandmother who took a small one, then to Aunt Dorothy whose face had turned flaming red and who said, "I think I'll just have vegetables tonight."

"I should hope so," my grandfather muttered.

"Oh, my dear," said Uncle Nicky. "Meat is essential to health. I am going to see to it that you take better care of your body from now on." He did not notice my grandfather glowering at him.

In spite of that faux pas and doubtless a few others, a couple of weeks later my grandfather held a proper wedding, the real one in his eyes, for his daughter and her blasted Hungarian, after which they set off for Geneva where Uncle Nicky was to finish his medical school.

Two weeks later, my grandparents, my Aunt Violet and I went to a garden party at the palace. I had been chosen to present a large bouquet of roses from our embassy garden to King Zog himself. I dressed up in my beautiful handmade Albanian costume: a delicate blouse sewn with silver and pearls, a rich, ruby-red velvet vest, a pair of white pantaloons with heavy blue cuffs, a pair of elaborate silver and blue shoes with great curled-up toes, and a circlet of daisies on my head.

We rode to the palace, its heavy gates opened by four soldiers who saluted and waved us on. "Is King Zog an evil king?" I whispered to Aunt Violet. "His palace looks like a prison."

"Well," Aunt Violet answered, "probably not evil but he's not much to write home about."

We rode on for a few more yards and then stopped at a big wall and got out of the car. Aunt Violet handed me the bouquet of roses to carry. The four of us proceeded through the garden entrance and there, at the far end of the garden, stood King Zog, erect and stiff beside my grandpa. He seemed to me to be smaller than a king should be and resplendent, not in proper robes and a crown, but in a uniform instead.

As Aunt Violet and I walked toward him, she bent toward me and whispered, "Curtsy to the king and give him your bouquet, Joyce."

I curtsied but, instead of the polite speech I had been taught to say, I blurted out, "Here's Grandma's flowers for you, Mr. King." And then, instead of handing over the bouquet, I just held on to it and stared at the king's many medals, golden eagles, crosses and epaulets. Finally, the king clicked his heels, nodded to me, bent down and pulled the flowers out of my hands.

"Curtsy again," Aunt Violet whispered, and I hastily did so.

As we turned away, I said in a loud whisper, "He doesn't look like a king at all. He looks like a toy soldier."

Aunt Violet hurried me out of the garden, desperately suppressing a fit of giggles. "Oh, lord," she said to my grandmother. "Out of the mouths of babes."

In the spring of 1931, around my sixth birthday, my Aunt Violet and I prepared to return to America. Before we got in the car to leave the American embassy, so Kemal could drive us to the coast on the way to Italy, I ran into the guard's house to say goodbye to Rassim.

"I have to go home now," I told him.

"I know," he said with a sad face. He lifted me into his lap, and I put my head on his chest and curled up tight against him. "We never gonna see each other no more, eh, little bossie?" Then he turned my face to his and gently kissed my forehead between my eyebrows. His lips were soft and tender; I could feel the rough tickle of his moustache. The kiss was moist and warm, a mark of grace. "Now I tell you something just for you, little bossie. You never let nobody kiss you there. That is Rassim's place forever and ever, for you to remember me by."

"Oh yes, Rassim," I said. "I promise." I felt filled with light.

"Time to go now," he said, and walked me to the waiting car.

As we pulled away, I climbed up onto the rear seat between Aunt Violet and Aunt Dorothy and stared out the back window, seeing it all one last time: the gleaming white embassy, the big black iron gates, my grandparents, the waving servants and Rassim, standing alone, his arm raised. His kiss lingered on my skin, protecting me forever. I watched them all grow smaller as I waved and waved, long after I could see them no more.

☙

Six weeks after I arrived in Chicago, my mother took me to visit her friend Rhea. For a while, I sat at the kitchen table reading while the two women chatted in the living room. Finally, bored, I wandered into the living room to join them.

"Little Shrub!" Rhea said. "Your mother tells me a man kissed you on the forehead and made you promise never to let anyone kiss you again on that oh-so-special spot."

"Yes," I said proudly. "Rassim kissed me right here." I pointed to the precious place on my forehead.

"Just like a man, wants exclusive rights," Rhea exclaimed, winking at my mother. Then she suddenly gripped my arms and pulled me to her and planted her hard, dry lips right on the spot of Rassim's kiss.

I could hardly breathe. I turned and took a step toward my mother, who sat calmly on the couch, not moving, her glance sliding over me. She and Rhea waggled their eyebrows at each other knowingly, the corners of their lips turning up in tiny smiles. Then my mother stood.

"Time to go home," she told me.

The Red Menace of Ravinia

From the time I got back to the States when I was six until I was 13 or 14, my parents were Communist believers.

Those were fertile times for radicals, the 1930s, a time when millions of unemployed Americans stood in breadlines for food, a time when the Dust Bowl made migrants of thousands of farm families and when, nearly 70 years after the Civil War, blacks were still an endangered people.

Every day throughout my childhood, I was reminded of what needed mending in America. Every day the mailman would bring us the *Communist Daily Worker* newspaper, every week the *Communist New Masses* magazine. Our house rang with my parents' outrage as they read about the latest unfairness perpetrated by the capitalist system. Almost every social occasion at our house meant loud arguments about whether FDR's reforms were going to save the country. The answer was always: how could they? It was still the same old capitalist system, wasn't it? Once or twice a year my parents would take me to a rally at some huge hall where Communist party leaders, a few union leaders and an occasional black writer would deliver passionate speeches about the rights of the working man and the noble work of our great Soviet brothers and sisters, as they stood beneath giant portraits of Lenin, Stalin and Marx.

I think my parents decided to become Communists during the time they lived on the west side of Chicago in the kind of working class and immigrant neighborhood that at that time nourished radicals of all stripes. My father, son of a blacksmith and farmer, lover of Walt Whitman and the common man, felt at home among working-class people. My mother, on the other hand, had grown up in an educated, upper-middle class family and, Communist though she might be in theory, hated living among the proletariat. She would become incensed at the way her neighbors elbowed their noisy way into her life.

The big hitch, however, in her being able to find an escape from the west side of Chicago was that we ourselves were almost as poor as our neighbors – my father made all of $22 a week as assistant director of the Jewish People's Institute.

But that wasn't going to stop my mother; nothing much ever did. She turned her eyes toward a string of jewel-like little towns that lay just north of Chicago along Lake Michigan: Evanston, Wilmette, Winnetka, Glencoe, Ravinia, Highland Park. She searched for months until she finally found a tiny artist's cottage (rent: $18 a month) in perhaps the most jewel-like town of them all, Ravinia. "But, damn it, I don't want to move," my outraged father told her. "Besides, here I can walk to work."

I was rooting for my mother. I didn't mind the West Side neighborhood so much; it was the school I hated. My first grade teacher was a sadistic lady who would stand at the head of the classroom with a long pointer in her hand, like some cruel Valkyrie with her spear. When one of us children wiggled in our seat or dropped a book, she would carefully point her pointer toward the offender, slowly lay her pointer down, pick up a ruler, walk over to him (it was almost always a him) and whack his hand as hard as she could. For lesser offenses, she would creep up behind us and rap us on the back of our heads with her knuckles.

We would try desperately to follow her directives while, out of the corners of our eyes, also track her trajectory around the room. Sometimes, if she came very close, we'd pee in our pants from fright, an offense that was punished first by a shaking and then standing in a corner with a dunce cap, wet pants and all. I began having nightmares every night. Every morning I would cry and beg my mother not to make me go to school. Every morning she would push me out the door, saying, "Oh, for God's sakes, she hasn't hit you."

So, when my father told my mother he wanted to stay

on the west side of Chicago because he could walk to work, I held my breath.

"Well, now you'll have the chance to read for an hour on the train," my mother said.

He knew it, and I knew it. We were moving.

By moving to Ravinia, we exchanged treeless dusty streets for a sanctuary of woods and ravines, neighbors' loud arguments for quiet, neat households, cruel teachers for kind ones, radical ferment for a Republican stronghold. Ah, but my mother knew all about Republicans: her parents were Republicans, her father a good friend of Herbert Hoover. Unlike my father, who sulked because he could no longer live side by side with his radical comrades, my mother girded her loins: she saw Ravinia as a worthy challenge.

I remember one of the first things she did to bring the light of radicalism to Ravinia. One Saturday, about six months after we'd moved there, my mother announced that my father was bringing a "mixed couple" from Chicago to visit.

They were to arrive by train that Saturday afternoon. Now, to tell you the truth, I wasn't quite sure what a "mixed couple" was and, since I was a little afraid to ask my mother – she tended to have contempt for those of us who were ignorant – I imagined that maybe they were . . . a mixed-up couple who had come to my parents to be straightened out. My mother was especially good at that.

My mother could have driven us the four blocks from our house to meet my father and this mixed couple at the railroad station, but she had no intention of depriving our neighbors of what promised to be a great educational experience. I don't know how many mixed couples there were in the United States back in 1933, but there could only have been a handful.

So we walked those four blocks to meet the train and watched as the mixed couple alighted: a handsome young black man, his timid white wife and their beautiful three-year-old son, Tuan. Then the six of us walked slowly the four blocks back to our house, past the stunned people peering through the windows of Hansons' drugstore and Zefir's family bakery, past every neighbor mowing his lawn or clipping her rose bushes. Most watched us surreptitiously; a few turned their backs and pretended they hadn't seen us at all, but every one of them knew something was happening in Ravinia that had never happened before. In Ravinia even the maids were white.

Our neighbors might have been disapproving but to their credit, they were fairly polite. Except, that is, for one neighbor, Mr. Swift.

Mr. Swift was some kind of big shot in the Republican party and tended to be outspoken and short-tempered, which is why, for a good part of my childhood, I connected being a staunch Republican with being a pissed-off Republican. When we reached his house, we saw that Mr. Swift was out there, scraping grass from between the flagstones of his front walk. He looked up at the mixed couple and said, "Good God, look at that, will you."

My father pretended he hadn't heard but my mother gave Mr. Swift her most withering look. The little white wife stumbled and her black husband put his arm around her.

At the time, I understood Mr. Swift's little cruelty toward this young couple, but it took me many years to recognize my mother's greater cruelty, having used them as her righteous lesson for her unenlightened neighbors.

There were other times when we invited blacks to Ravinia: my father once brought the famous black folksinger, Josh White, to our house, along with some other Chicago radicals, and we all listened to his songs and sang some with him. And once a group of both black and white aspiring writers, who had taken a literature class taught by my father, spent the afternoon with us. I remember one of them telling us his uncle had been lynched for trying to get some money owed him by a white man. Oh, I knew what lynching was, alright. It was in the *Daily Worker* that I had first seen a photograph of a lynched black man, his neck all twisted to one side, his hands tied with rope, hanging from a tree. I was eight years old when I saw that picture and until then I hadn't known that people did such terrible things to other people.

Whatever our Ravinia neighbors may have thought about these Negro and working-class invasions, they mostly talked about them behind closed doors. But at school one day, Mr. Swift's son, Tommy, stopped me on the playground, poked my chest hard and said, "Your mother and father are ba-ad. And you, you're bad too."

A wave of shame swept over me. I cast my eyes down at the ground until he went away but the feel of his hard finger lingered as though a bullet had lodged there. When I went home I asked my mother, "Why do people think Communists are bad?"

"Because we threaten them," she told me with a little smile. "People on top are always afraid of being toppled."

I wasn't sure my mother was right. Oh, I knew Tommy Swift was on top alright – he was one of the handsomest boys in our class as well as a good athlete – but I couldn't picture him being afraid of anything, let alone being toppled.

My mother tried other ways to infiltrate her fellow Ravinians. She would attend library lectures, school teas, concerts, searching for interesting women and then, when she had selected a possibility, she would exert all her charm to make that woman her friend. In this fashion, she gathered around her a network of educated, liberal and bored middle-class women who found her radical beliefs exciting. My parents sometimes attended parties at their homes and I would tag along since we had no money for a babysitter. I'd sit in a corner, pretending to read my book, but all the time watching and listening.

The women would usually gather around my handsome, poetic-looking father as he earnestly discussed the merits of some radical book or, better yet, recited the poetry of Walt Whitman or, best of all, sang Russian folksongs in his rich baritone. My mother possessed a kind of fragile prettiness that led men to want to protect her and invariably underestimate her stiletto intellect. She would first flirt with her friends' husbands and then challenge them in her politically provocative way that almost always ended with her besting them. I remember one of the husbands once exasperatedly saying to her, "Tell me, Hilda, since you think we're all a bunch of awful capitalists, what the hell are you doing here in the middle of the enemy camp? Why aren't you marching with the workers of the world?"

"Why, Henry," my mother replied, with a tiny smile, "don't you see? I'm marching toward you in this battlefield and aiming right for your enemy heart," and then blew him a kiss.

My mother started a radical book discussion group and

a current events discussion group. She organized trips into Chicago to see left-wing plays. And finally she suggested her friends take the devil by the horns and accompany her to a Communist party rally.

The particular Communist rally my mother had in mind was no ordinary one. This one was going to showcase the great Paul Robeson giving a speech and singing a new song, "Ballad for Americans." Apprehensive as my mother's friends might have been, most of them also wanted her approval, so all but one of them went. They all became visibly anxious as we walked into that big hall, especially when we all had to start off the rally by singing "The Internationale" – hundreds of rough, out-of-tune voices bellowing, "Arise ye prisoners of starvation, Arise ye wretched of the earth, For justice thunders condemnation, A better world's in birth."

But then, when at last Robeson filled the hall with his deep and powerful voice singing "Ballad for Americans," all of us in the audience ecstatically swayed and cried and cheered so hard Robeson had to sing it again. And my mother's friends declared it was one of the most splendid evenings of their lives.

"Yeah," my mother said later to my father with her usual cynicism. "They were so relieved I hadn't made them swear allegiance to the Communist cause." But I could tell she was pleased.

Yet, hard as my parents worked to move members of our community to the left (and I think they might have succeeded a little), Ravinia's Rock of Republicanism still stood, solid as ever. When the 1936 election results were tallied, somewhere over 200 people in Ravinia had voted for the Republican candidate Alf Landon. About 120

Democrats voted for Franklin Delano Roosevelt. Two (friends of my parents) voted for Norman Thomas, the Socialist candidate.

And only two, my parents, voted for Earl Browder, the Communist candidate.

Jimmy Wonnell, Oh Jimmy Wonnell

The second great love of my life after Rassim appeared to me in fourth grade at Ravinia Elementary School. I fell in love with Jimmy Wonnell. And I stayed in love with Jimmy Wonnell until we both graduated from eighth grade and I never saw him again nor ever heard anything more about him. I suppose there's still a tiny bit of my heart that's in love with Jimmy Wonnell.

Jimmy Wonnell was not much of a student at Ravinia Elementary School but he was handsome, athletic, had a delightful chuckle, loved life, was basically decent and was admired by almost all of us. In the classroom, he kept the day from being dull. When he couldn't answer the teacher's question, which was fairly often, he had a debonair way of taking a brave guess. We all rooted for him though we all knew that the likelihood of his guessing correctly was miniscule. Though he was a mischievous boy he was never mean.

For weeks, I would wait with bated breath to have him pay any attention to me. And then, one day, out of the blue, it would happen. He would lean over toward me on his way to his seat, yank one of my pigtails and whisper, "I'm gonna dip your pigtail in the inkwell, Joycie!"

Even though I knew he wouldn't and I was now in heaven, I would invariably yell, "Teacher, teacher, Jimmy says he's gonna . . . "

"Yes, Joyce. Jimmy, now stop it," she'd say with a weary little smile, and then move his seat so it was far, far away from me.

Jimmy would chuckle and go back to trying to do our arithmetic lesson. I, on the other hand, couldn't think straight for a day or two because, at last, Jimmy Wonnell had noticed me. But then I would realize that I should have kept my mouth shut. Now he would be far, far away from me for the rest of the semester! And I knew that actually it was I who was probably the dumber of the two of us.

Jimmy Wonnell was always chosen to be captain of one of our teams, no matter which sport we were playing: baseball, soccer, volleyball. Everybody wanted to be on Jimmy Wonnell's team because it almost always won. Jimmy played hard. Jimmy played fast. Jimmy always played fairly and with grace.

During spring and fall, we had our gym periods outdoors. The two captains of our teams got to take turns choosing who they wanted on their team. The teachers made sure that every single one of us, boys and girls alike, were chosen in the end. There were two kids who were always picked first. Captain Jimmy Wonnell always picked a boy from a poor family across the tracks; Oscar was his name. Oscar was slow on the uptake and his facial features made him look a bit like some kind of Neanderthal. And what made him look even more like a Neanderthal was that his arms hung down well below his knees. I have never seen that in anyone in all my life except in Oscar. Oscar was immensely strong but at the same time gentle. He had failed fourth grade twice but made it the third time. Yet, those of us on Jimmy's team were always grateful that we had slow Oscar on our side because Dennis, the other team's first pick, was just a mean big kid who we all hated. We never hated Oscar.

I was always picked next to last, except once. Two of us girls: Clarice Deffenbaugh (who was fat, dumb and slow as molasses) and me (who was tiny, awkward and forever scared – that I would get some bigger kid's elbow smashing into my face), we two were the absolute dregs who finally had to be reluctantly chosen as part of one or the other team. Only once did Jimmy Wonnell hurt my feelings by choosing Clarice Deffenbaugh as his last teammate, leaving me standing there as the least desired by anyone.

I hated sports. I was an absolute dunce at every single physical activity we ever did at that wonderful school. If I wasn't getting smashed with a ball or an elbow, I was getting trampled underfoot, missing the catch, or just generally being weak, tiny and uncoordinated.

Except once.

It was a dark and dreary day in the winter of 1937. I was 12 years old, in the eighth grade and out of excuses to miss gym. To make things worse, our gym teacher, Mr. Granton, was introducing some complicated new game I was sure to be hopeless at, some sort of amalgam of baseball and soccer with a bit of basketball thrown in. I was doomed.

When you came up to bat in this game, you were supposed to punch the volleyball hard with your fist, then run like hell through the opposing team who were, of course, trying to get the ball so they could wham you with it before you touched the back wall, the safety zone. The only good thing for you if you were the runner was that no one out in the field was allowed to take their feet off the ground. They could only spin their upper bodies as far as possible while their feet remained immobile. Any player who moved one of his feet was tossed out of the game and, as the game proceeded, usually at least half the team in the field wound up getting knocked out.

But even if you, the runner, were lucky enough to reach the back wall without being hit, you couldn't stay there forever. No such luck. You had to run back through what was left of the opposing team to home plate without letting anyone hit you with the ball. You not only had to run, but you had to do it swiftly, warily, while constantly changing directions, dodging one player after another. With only the bigger, stronger players remaining on the field, it seemed the perfect set-up for my demise.

Being the littlest and weakest, the one everybody knew

had no physical ability whatsoever, I had been put up to bat last, with the hope that 1) the other team would have lost so many members from illegally moving their feet and 2) my team would have gained so many points that 3) I would turn out to be extraneous. But by the time my turn came up, the teams were even, so it was clear: I was going to lose the game for us.

I, of course, did everything wrong. I punched the ball and it just barely made it over the line, then bounced off to one side. I just stood there, thinking it was a foul. My team yelled, "Run!" So I ran. I knew I could only be hit by someone with the ball in hand so I ran crazily.

"Run, Joyce, run!" they yelled. I ran to the right, I ran to the left, got confused and started back to base. "Wrong direction!" they screamed. So I twirled around and ran to the wall. And just made it before I was hit. Safe! There I was, at that back wall. I knew very well I would never make it back.

I began my long run from the wall to the base past the few enemies still left on the floor. Somehow, no one was paying much attention to me. My guess is that the opposing team assumed I was an easy target and had relaxed, thinking someone else would take care of me for good. Suddenly I became filled, for the first and perhaps only time in my life, with the conviction that I was both brave and certain of what I should do. I was going make it back to home plate untouched and win this game for my team.

I ran, I swerved, I ducked, I dodged. And then I did something no one else in my class could have done because I was so tiny. There in front of me was huge George Fenster, standing with his legs spread wide apart and his back to me, waiting to have the ball thrown to him so he could clobber me. George Fenster was in the eighth grade, like me, but he was already six feet tall with long, long legs – a sort of absent-minded Colossus. An instant before someone thought to throw George the ball, I crouched and dove between his legs, then sped for home. In astonishment, George Fenster dropped the ball as soon as he got it. It rolled half-heartedly along the floor. No one picked it up. There was a moment of silence.

Then everyone, on both teams, cheered me on with wild, surprised screams while poor George just stood there with his mouth wide open in shock and I touched home base.

And as I did, Jimmy Wonnell picked me up and set me on his shoulder and pranced with me around the whole gymnasium in a victory dance as everyone, even our gym teacher, clapped and roared and followed us in a long conga line.

So yes, Jimmy Wonnell, I still love you and I always will.

Thyra

After 15 unhappy years together, my parents split up when I was in high school. I first met my father's second wife, Thyra Edwards, in 1939 when I was 14. She and my father had gotten to know each other when they'd both moved into the same settlement house for social workers on the South Side of Chicago, where my father was, by now, the Director of the Jewish People's Institute. Thyra had just returned from a workshop and lecture series she had given down in Mexico as part of her dedication to training social workers around the world.

My father fell in love with Thyra. On the surface, you might wonder why. Not because she was black and he was white. That didn't matter to my father. But what did matter was that Thyra was seven years older than my father, who was then in his late 30s. My father had always admired youth and spent a great deal of time staying young himself through exercise and careful diet. In addition, Thyra was suffering from one of a string of illnesses she'd been plagued with throughout her life and my father, up till then, was a man who hated being near sick people.

But it didn't take long for anyone who got to know my future stepmother to admire her character and appreciate her integrity, her compassion and her courage. My father was simply bowled over by her. She was the best thing that ever happened to him, though I'm not sure he ever admitted that to anyone, even himself.

There were, of course, only a handful of black-white marriages back then, so that meant there was a great deal of disapproval for what they had dared to do, even in big northern cities like Chicago and New York. But they faced that disapproval – my father all too often with an angry scowl; my stepmother with her usual grace and dignity. I remember walking down a sidewalk with them one afternoon in Chicago when several people showed their disgust by spitting at us, taking up the whole sidewalk so we had to walk in the street and one old lady saying, "Jaysus, Mary and Joseph. Look at that, will ya."

They moved to New York City a couple of years later

when Thyra was offered a job as an investigative reporter for a Harlem newspaper, *The Amsterdam News,* and she supported my father while he looked for a job. I happened to be visiting them on summer break from college when one day Thyra asked me to come with her to find a better apartment. "I think it's only fair for landlords to know we're a white-Negro family," she told me.

I still remember the last place we went to that day. After Thyra asked the landlord if we could see the apartment he had for rent, he turned to me and said, "Little white gal, you get yourself and your monkey outta here."

Just as I had indignantly started to set this man straight, my stepmother took my elbow, turned me around and, arm-in-arm, we slowly and with dignity walked out of there.

After Thyra found a great apartment near Washington Square and filled it with all the beautiful things she had collected from around the world, my father decided it was time to invite his brothers and sisters, all of whom lived in or near Hartford, Connecticut, to come down to New York City for a party to welcome Thyra into our family.

My father and my stepmother never quarreled, even when they differed. My father could be stubborn at times but Thyra had a gentle way of getting him to see the light. Well, it didn't work this time. She had wanted my father to wait so his siblings could get more used to the idea of having a Negro as part of our family. But he had said, "By God, right is right," and it was time his family faced that.

The big question that hung in the air was: Who Would Come and Who Wouldn't.

Not my fun-loving Uncle Jim who told clever jokes, was a great dancer, used to bounce me on his knee when I was little and call me his Juicy Joycey. Not my sweet Aunt Mary who, when I was 14 and living with her, once stayed up almost all night to finish sewing me a ball gown to wear to my first dance. Certainly not my stern Aunt Ida who worked so hard not only running her farm but also a little country store and wouldn't think of wasting her time to meet some colored woman who must be crazy anyway to go and marry her *meshuggeneh* brother. And not either my Uncle Max nor my Aunt Beatie who just didn't want to think about what their brother had gone and done.

The youngest in the family, my Uncle Bernie, the one who owned a highly successful sporting goods store, wondered why would it be so bad to just go and meet the woman. He almost came, until his wife, my Aunt Ruth, reminded my Uncle Bernie that if word ever got out that he had a Negro sister-in-law, he'd never ever again be able to play golf at his country club. Didn't he remember how hard it had been to get into that country club because he was a Jew? And besides, she wouldn't have a single friend left to play canasta with, let alone talk to her.

So, after dozens of frantic phone calls back and forth up there in Hartford, the upshot was that none of my father's brothers or sisters, all of whom I loved and some of whom I admired, were willing to come down to New York to meet "that woman."

Even at our wisest we are all of us combinations of courage and cowardice, kindness and cruelty.

There was, however, one lone family member who eventually made the trip from Hartford to New York. She was my favorite, Aunt Anya, my Uncle Max's second wife, the one who had raised his two children, the one who had gone back to nursing to support the family when Uncle Max's hardware store failed, the one who always calmed everyone's escalating nerves whenever one sister-in-law got mad at another sister-in-law. Force of nature that she was, my dear Aunt Anya had been unable to move a single other family member to overcome their fear of the alien who had invaded our family.

Aunt Anya and Thyra began a quiet relationship by talking on the phone once a week. And one day Aunt Anya boarded the bus to New York, came to my father's and Thyra's apartment, and their friendship lasted until Thyra died.

At the end of World War II, my father was offered a job by the American Jewish Joint Distribution Committee to become Director of Operations for all the Jewish refugee camps in Italy. He almost didn't get the job. The board of directors of the AJDC liked my father's background and they had been delighted when my father had described his wife's wonderful background. "Ah," said one of the board members, "it looks as though we're getting two for the price of one."

Everyone laughed, except my father. "However, I must tell you that my wife is a Negro. I am proud to say that she was recently heralded as one of the most outstanding Negro women in the world for her remarkable years of doing social work to help the poor of Africa, Asia and South America."

There was a stunned silence and then the chairman thundered, "Are you telling us you are married to a Negro woman? Because you have to realize that, good woman as I'm sure your wife must be, it is simply impossible for you to take her with you to Italy as a representative of the AJDC."

My father answered, "You would ask me to care for our

fellow Jews who have been ostracized, terrorized, beaten and murdered, and then you would have me turn my back on my wife simply because she is a Negro, one of a race that has been ostracized, terrorized, beaten and murdered in our country? If this is your offer, then no, I won't accept your job."

This has always seemed to me to have been my father's finest hour.

About a week later, after quite a bit of wrangling among the board members, the AJDC agreed to permit Thyra to accompany my father to Italy.

There was, at first, some confusion about Thyra among the refugees in those camps. The Director's wife must be a Jew, right? After all, she's married to the Director who is, for sure, a Jew. But whoever saw a Jew who looked like that? Soon, however, it didn't really matter what she was. Thyra worked so tirelessly to better the lives of the women and children in those camps that, when the refugees finally recognized her great dedication to them and the word began to spread, she became famously known throughout all the camps as Our Black Jew.

Both my father and Thyra worked very hard during those years in Italy. Periodically, Thyra would become ill again – often with painful arthritis and then, twice, with pneumonia. She would rest a while, then go back to work, driving herself even harder, especially to help the children.

One of the most difficult and harrowing parts of the work my father and stepmother did was to help some of the refugees get to Israel, which was the goal of the majority. British ships at that time were trying to keep new immigrants from entering Israel. So what my father, Thyra and other members of the staff had to do was load these refugees into trucks at night, take them to some obscure harbors along the east coast of Italy and board them onto small, swift boats in the hope that these boats could evade the British warships waiting for them at the eastern end of the Mediterranean. Not all of these boats made it, but many of them did.

In 1953, as she was setting up a child care program in Rome for the refugee children, Thyra discovered she had breast cancer. "I can't help but be angry at my fragile body," she wrote my Aunt Anya. "I am so deeply tired but I must finish my work here." By the time she and my father finally left Italy and returned to New York it was too late.

No good hospital (that is, for whites only) would take Thyra as a patient. As Thyra became very ill, my father found a nursing home for Negroes in Brooklyn run by two women who were fine, caring people but had no nurses' training, two black women caring for about a dozen dying black women in one large room. Thyra died there late one night with none of us by her side.

There was a memorial service for her at a church in Harlem. At the service, one of Thyra's sisters told of what life had been like when they were children in Texas and how Thyra, the oldest of four girls, had been sick so often that their mother once told her The Lord had chosen her to take on their whole family's pain because He knew she was the most determined girl in the world and would succeed no matter what. And, said her sister, The Lord had been right! We all smiled at that.

The poets Langston Hughes and Gwendolyn Brooks each read a poem they'd written for her.

Thyra's closest friend, the jazz pianist Hazel Scott, played a special piece for her and then accompanied Paul Robeson as he sang a hymn to the woman he called "a strong, gentle and remarkable soul."

Many years later, I met a man who had been one of the refugee children who had tried to reach Israel and who remembered Thyra. "I remember three things about her," he told me, "her beautiful bronze face, her great kindness to us all and, most of all, that when my family was about to board the boat, she pressed into my hand a little wooden horse and told me, 'This horse will help you find a good life.'"

They didn't make it to Israel, he told me. They were caught and interned by the British. Eventually the family made it to the United States. "I wish your stepmother was still alive," the man told me, "so I could tell her that, yes, I have had a good life. And I still have that wooden horse."

And I still have some bits of Thyra's life with me too. Hanging above my living room there is a beautiful Persian rug draped over a balcony wall. In my front hall lies another of her rugs, this one from the Caucasus. And on my desk sits a book about Thyra Edwards called *Black Activist in the Global Freedom Struggle.*

How I Got to College

By the time I was a senior in high school, I was an arrogant little snot. I was part of a group of others like myself, five or six arrogant boys and girls. We were terrible at sports and socially inept. What we really excelled at was encouraging each other's intellectual pretensions, which included, of course, sneering at our sub-human fellow students. Privately, we sneered a bit at each other, too.

I, for example, would often wonder how much better and more intelligent than these wannabes my college friends would turn out to be. Would we be tossing lines of T. S. Eliot's "The Love Song of J. Alfred Prufrock" back and forth? Staying up night after night passionately discussing Nietszche's philosophy until we understood him better than any Berkeley student who had ever been there before us?

I was headed for Berkeley from my hometown of Chicago. The year was 1942. I had packed a handsome but heavy leather suitcase reluctantly given to me by my father. (My father was a bit of a dandy who carefully selected only the best of everything, or at least the best he could afford. It was his second-best suitcase and he knew he'd never see it again.) I had stuffed it with all my summer clothes and half my winter clothes, plus five of the most important books in my life. And I could hardly lift the damn thing.

I had won my *Webster's Collegiate Dictionary* in an English Department contest by beating out the boy we all knew was going to be the valedictorian of our class and whom I had a big crush on. I had apparently so damaged his ego by winning that he could hardly speak to me for a couple of weeks. Well, I felt awful but I wasn't going to pretend I was sorry. Since I had to show him I didn't care, I deliberately made a date with this rich boy who was rather disgusting but who owned a huge, shiny black convertible.

As you'd expect, it wasn't the greatest date in the world. I got a little drunk, he got a little drunk and then I let him give me this sloppy, wet kiss. Yech. When he took me to the door of the apartment where my mother and I lived, he asked if he could take me out again. I said, "Never." His head jerked as though I'd socked him and I learned that boys with big convertibles can get their feelings hurt just as easily as boys with big intellects.

But a week later my valedictorian heartthrob and I began speaking to each other again. Though I was never able to get him to kiss me, he at least did once hold my hand and majestically address me as "my dear child."

I was taking along my second book, *A Treasury of Modern Poetry*, because I was hell-bent on knocking the socks off my future fellow intellects by reciting from memory the whole of "The Love Song of J. Alfred Prufrock." As college got closer, I began to panic a little because I could never get through the poem without screwing up at least a couple of lines or, at times, even dropping whole chunks of it. I still can't.

My third book was one of Dostoevsky's, the first piece of really great literature I'd read at age 13. The depths of Dostoevsky's monumental suffering spoke to my own singular adolescent despair. I'm not talking here about *Crime and Punishment*. No, no. More bitter than that. It was Dostoevsky's tale of his imprisonment in Siberia, *The House of the Dead*, that had pierced my heart. Plus, I admit, it made me hope that I could be admired for reading a Dostoevsky that probably no one else had even heard of.

My fourth book was a deep, deep tome, a lot of which I didn't understand at all. But that didn't stop me. I understood enough of it to confidently explain to anybody who would listen what was the deep, deep meaning of their behavior: why Freddie told his stupid bathroom jokes, why Mary Ellen always had to be right, why our English teacher Mr. Lippman made those pathetic attempts to get us all to love him. I could even tell everybody why it was all our parents' fault. Yep, *The Collected Works of Sigmund Freud*. My heaviest book, in every respect.

It was my fifth book that I was worried about. *Small Fry and the Winged Horse* was its name. It was a book of Greek mythology. The winged horse was the great god Pegasus. I was worried because it was a children's book. I had treasured it ever since my eighth birthday. Bringing a children's book to college seemed like still sucking my thumb.

I was 17 but looked about 10 or 11. So my mother saved money by buying me a half-fare ticket for the train to San Francisco. "She's got someone waiting for her at the other end," my mother lied to the stationmaster because she knew the railroad required underage kids to be accompanied by an adult. When he fell for it, she sent me on my way. "Ask for directions when you get there. Remember, you've only got enough money for the first semester. After that you're on your own. Good luck."

I knew, from long experience, plus the weary way she said "good luck," that she was convinced I didn't have what it took to make it through college. Or any part of life, for that matter.

As I climbed into the train, the reality hit me that I had very little idea of what to expect once the train ride was over nor, to be more practical, how to even find my way to Berkeley from San Francisco. Colleges were not in the least parental back in those days. Nor were my parents. So none of them had tried to clear the way for me.

Because we were at the beginning of World War II, almost all of our most modern trains that summer had been commandeered for our brave troops who were being moved across America either east to the European theatre of operations to fight the Germans or west to the Pacific Ocean to fight the Japanese. That meant that those of us who weren't soldiers rode in what was leftover railroad stock, hauled out of old depots and repaired as best the railroad companies could. My guess is that the train I rode on must have dated from sometime in the late 19th century. It had the most uncomfortable seats imaginable – slippery, rigid and shaped to conform to no known human body. There was, of course, no air conditioning. One ceiling fan per railroad car wheeled its creaky, desultory way. The train had dim, dusty windows that couldn't be opened and wrought-iron transoms that couldn't be closed. And since it also had a coal-fired engine, cinders and ashes would float down on us through those open transoms until, within a few hours, we all became black with soot and sweat.

The railroad cars were not only old, they were far too few in number. There were so many people on the train that about a quarter of them had to sit in the aisles on their suitcases until we got to Des Moines, Iowa. During the first hour, a pungent perfume was added to our woes when a little boy announced, "Mommy, I feel sick," and vomited all over her and himself.

By the second day, the bad news was that the dining car had been removed without explanation, almost every toilet on the train had stopped flushing and none of the bathroom sinks produced water. The good news was that the train made an infinite number of stops where we could all rush out to use the station bathrooms, rush to buy food and drink, and then wearily climb back onto the train before it could pull out without us. Which it did once, heedless of the despairing cries of a couple it left stranded in a small town in Nebraska.

On and on and on we stopped and started, sometimes

making way for those troop trains which always had priority: four days and three nights that felt like 40 days and 39 nights.

When at last we reached San Francisco, we weary travelers were a filthy, bedraggled and sleepless mess. Eventually I found the bus going across the Bay Bridge to Berkeley, only to discover, once I got off it, that the campus lay a mile up from the bus station.

It was nearly four in the afternoon. So I began my journey up the hill, trying desperately to reach campus before the college offices closed for the day, dragging my leaden suitcase behind me and stopping every few yards to rest. It was getting so late I began to think that, once I reached the campus, I might have to search for some out-of-the-way bush to sleep under. And, while part of me imagined strange, dangerous, lurking men ravishing me there in the middle of the night, another part of me had a kind of what-the-hell feeling because any semblance of a bed I could actually stretch my body out onto now seemed to me a glorious miracle.

By now, I had started walking through one of Berkeley's quiet, suburban-ish neighborhoods. As I passed a house, I noticed a large, flowing bush in its front yard near the sidewalk. Tired as I was, I did not crawl under it and go to sleep. Instead, peering around to be sure no one saw me, I opened my suitcase and removed all my winter clothes and all my books, except for *Small Fry and the Winged Horse*. Wrapping the books in my winter jacket, I stuffed everything under the bush, then made sure I remembered the address. (And I remember it to this day: 321 Weber Drive.) My heart heavy but my suitcase lighter, I set off again and miraculously made it to the campus offices before they closed.

There were no campus dorms in those days. I needed cheap accommodations. The closest and cheapest one was a co-op house (room and board: $33 plus 25 hours of housework per month) and it lay up the hill beyond the campus.

So I dragged myself seven more bloody blocks into the Berkeley hills and finally knocked on the door of a large, shabby, white-shingled house. A tall, angular woman opened the door. "I'm the student they just called you about for a room," I said. She stared down at me.

"You've got to be kidding," she said. "You're just a baby."

"I'm 17," I said.

"Well, you could have fooled me," she said.

I was ready for bed but she made me stand there, swaying, in the front hall while she not only advised me of the house rules but also threatened me with dire consequences if I broke them. Then she took me upstairs to meet my roommate. I confess I had pictured another freshman with whom I could share my deep thoughts and delicate soul, or at least, if she wasn't up to my high standards, to whom I could give sage advice. Instead, my roommate turned out to be nearly 10 years older than I was. Grace was Berkeley's first-ever woman mining engineering graduate student. And she wasn't about to share her soul, if she had one, with the likes of me.

"Let's get things clear from the git-go," she told me as I stood, still swaying, in the middle of the room. "You do things my way."

And that was, indeed, what I did. Grace's way meant keeping my mouth shut when she broke house rules by sneaking out the window every night to meet her boyfriend. Grace's way was keeping my mouth shut when she stole food from the fridge. And one night, Grace's way was my finding another place to sleep when her boyfriend was so drunk that she got him to climb through the window into our room so he could sleep in my bed.

I did eventually come close to perceiving Berkeley as the place of my highest ideals. Once I had rescued my clothes and my four books from under that bush, I gradually found classmates with whom I could discuss the glories of T.S. Eliot, Nietzsche, Freud and Dostoevsky, as well as discover a pantheon of new gods.

One night, sometime that first year at Berkeley, I had a dream, a familiar one from my childhood, yet changed. In my dream I had climbed onto the back of Pegasus, my great, golden mythological winged horse. But instead of flying high above the world's great oceans, mountains and deserts, this time we flew over the Berkeley campus while all the students and professors stared up at us in stunned amazement. It was the last time I ever dreamt my Pegasus dream.

Back on earth, I gradually worked out how to support myself by becoming an artist's model and a switchboard operator. Learned enough of the Russian language to read Dostoevsky aloud in the original. Learned much more about the glories of the 19th century Russian writers: Tolstoy, Gogol, Pushkin, Chekhov, Turgenev. Also acquired the knack of whipping round and round my Russian history professor's desk and out the door of his office before he could catch me for a kiss and a feel. Took delight in finding a few good friends to talk Nietzsche and Freud with and foolishly admired some pretentious fakers. Found love and then saw that it wasn't. And narrowly saved myself from the precipice of life time and time again.

And, when you think of it, what else is college for?

My Hungarian Uncle

Let me start by saying that my Uncle Nicky was tall. In our family, this was no minor matter. For as far back as anyone could remember, not a single man or woman in our family had ever reached any higher than five feet, six inches, including the patriarch of our family, my grandfather, who had been a fairly famous foreign correspondent for the *New York Times* and was the ambassador to Albania.

From the soles of his always-elegant shoes to the top of his magnificent head of thick black wavy hair, my Uncle Nicky towered above us all at six feet, one and a half inches.

Not only was he a giant among men, but my Uncle Nicky was extraordinarily handsome and had this soft, smooth way of curling his Hungarian tongue around the English language that made women weak. The other men in my mother's family weren't as handsome but they were highly intelligent – intellectuals actually – but once women got a gander at my Uncle Nicky, they just tossed intellectualism overboard.

I think what stunned everyone was that it was my Aunt Dorothy, of all people, who had captured this exotic creature. And what stunned them even more was how she managed to do it.

My Aunt Dorothy was my mother's next younger sister and after meeting her in Albania during my youthful sojourn there, she had become my favorite aunt on that side of the family. She was a bit naïve, sweet, kind and gentle. But she was no great beauty and a bit of a goody-two-shoes. My grandparents could always count on Dorothy to do the right thing.

On top of all that, all the women in my mother's family had been raised with a rather strait-jacketed approach to matters of the flesh. I still remember my grandmother telling me, with some pride, that despite 30 years of marriage and four children, my grandfather had never seen her naked. So you might say that, when my Uncle Nicky entered into this family, it was a little like having Rudolf Valentino stride across the desert and lift up the flap of their Girl Scout tent.

I was there when their romance began and in fact played

a key role in bringing my Aunt Dorothy and my Uncle Nicky together.

Back in 1930, after my ship crossing with the flappers, opera singers and chicken-and-ice-cream breakfasts, I had been retrieved in Paris by my two aunts, Dorothy and Violet. We were slowly wending our way across Europe, headed for Albania. One of our stops was the home of a college classmate of my Aunt Dorothy's in Geneva, Switzerland, where she was having a dance party for my aunts. At that party was this young, handsome Hungarian student surrounded by adoring young women.

Things didn't start off all that well for my Aunt Dorothy. My future Uncle Nicky danced once with her but not again. From then on, Aunt Dorothy just sat, stunned, and stared at him with burning intensity. Burning intensity and my Aunt Dorothy had never met each other before. When my more popular Aunt Violet stopped for a second to ask her what was the matter, Dorothy whispered, "He's beautiful and he's nice too – and I don't think he's going to want to dance with me ever again."

I sat next to poor, miserable Aunt Dorothy, bored to tears and getting mad at this man who was making her so unhappy. So, after a while, I got up and did what pretty much any five-year-old might do. I crossed the room, poked him on his leg and yelled up to him, "You come dance with my Aunt Dorothy again!"

Well, everybody laughed, he pulled one of my pigtails. Oh, I always hated that and it made me really mad so I said, "You big stupid," and I kicked him.

At that point, he picked me up and carried me across the room to Aunt Dorothy. "Does she belong to you?" he asked, a smile playing on his luscious lips.

Poor Aunt Dorothy's face was flaming red. "Yes, she's my niece. I'm so sorry if she hurt you."

"Hurt me?" he said. "Ha. It was a tiny nothing." And then he bowed and asked her to dance.

Even though Aunt Dorothy wasn't much of a dancer (she had bad feet), some kind of impossible magic must have happened between them because two days later it was only my Aunt Violet and I who set off for Albania. Aunt Dorothy had wangled an invitation from her friend to stay on in Geneva for two or three more weeks.

It didn't take long for my grandfather to uncover this romance, so he set about investigating this highly suspect young man. What he found was that, though Nicky was a medical student, not to be sneered at in a potential son-in-law, and was perhaps a bright young fellow, since the Hungarian government was paying for all his medical training, not only did Nicky come from a poor peasant family who lived in some godforsaken Hungarian village but, even worse, he had a reputation as a notorious Don Juan, one who particularly liked having affairs with married women because they didn't expect anything permanent from him. Which, of course, made my grandfather wonder what this rapscallion might have been doing with what he hoped was still his virginal daughter.

When my Aunt Dorothy finally reached Albania, my grandfather laid down the law to her and she dutifully replied, "Yes, Father." And that, seemingly, was that.

But not quite. For the first and perhaps only time in her life, my gentle, obedient Aunt Dorothy became devious. She hatched a plot to leave her dear papa behind and set off on an all-woman road trip with Aunt Violet and with my innocent grandmother as chaperone to visit some of the other charming Middle European countries, one of which just happened to be Hungary where my future Uncle Nicky just happened to be on vacation in his little village, which they just happened to drive through and just happened to have car trouble which necessitated their staying for the night. And, by the time my grandmother began to understand what was happening, my Aunt Dorothy and my Uncle Nicky had gotten married at the village registry office. After which the whole village exploded in an orgy of feasting including lots and lots to drink, with all the men taking turns dancing Aunt Dorothy round and round until finally she had to run behind a bush and throw up, which set the men to teasing my Uncle Nicky about what a sorry wedding night he was about to have.

He just smiled, lifted her up and disappeared with her in his arms.

Back in Albania, my outraged grandfather did his best to re-establish family control by holding his own wedding for his daughter, a proper, white-lace wedding with the king of Albania, King Zog, attending. The next week Aunt Dorothy and Uncle Nicky left hastily for Geneva.

Well, to the surprise of everyone, in the next few years my Uncle Nicky seemed to live up to our family's uptight standards. After he'd finished his medical training, Uncle Nicky and Aunt Dorothy moved to Los Angeles where he set up what became a highly successful family practice. Women especially found my uncle to be a deeply, deeply understanding doctor.

And then my Uncle Nicky did something that stunned

everyone in our family. Starting around 1936 or 7 until he was forced to stop at the beginning of WWII, Uncle Nicky saved the lives of nearly 40 members of his family, all of them Hungarian Jews, from almost certain death in the Nazi concentration camps. He rescued his elderly parents, his four brothers and two sisters, their spouses and children, some cousins, aunts and uncles. He found ways to bring them all to America, set them up in apartments, paid for their rent and food until they found work and saw to it they became US citizens. They were a loud, raucous band of gypsies, so there was a little tension on our family's part when the two families met each other but, of course, it was my Aunt Dorothy, being who she was, who chose to bear the brunt of it all.

Then after that, my Uncle Nicky seemed to just settle down into typical American middle class life. Occasionally, when I'd come down from Berkeley to visit them during my wild college days, he would take me off to a corner and tell me a few tales of his wild bachelor days. And I would think to myself: Poor, poor Uncle Nicky. How can he bear the dullness of his life? Who would have guessed he'd turn out this way? Yet I knew that, of all the marriages in my mother's family, my Aunt Dorothy and my Uncle Nicky had by far the happiest one.

Then one day about 20 years into their marriage, Aunt Dorothy discovered a little red book sitting on top of my Uncle Nicky's desk, a little red book that contained the names of the hundreds of women he'd been sleeping with during their marriage, including the dates on which the trysts had occurred.

My Aunt Dorothy confronted him and asked him why

he had done it. When had he stopped loving her?

And all my Uncle Nicky could reply was, "Oh, no, I love you deeply. Why did I do it? I suppose because . . . because it was so easy."

So my Aunt Dorothy left my Uncle Nicky. Oh, he tried to woo her back in all kinds of ways, including buying her a beautiful home way up in the Hollywood Hills next to Griffith Park but she refused to be bought.

And then, after about five or six years, my Aunt Dorothy did come back to him, perhaps for the only reason that could have persuaded her: my Uncle Nicky got lung cancer. So they lived together in that big house, she nursed him devotedly and they fell in love again.

Their 25-year-old son, my cousin Alex, and I came together from the East Coast to visit them. Sitting up in bed, my Uncle Nicky still looked handsome. When we left him to take a nap while we sat in the kitchen, my cousin, who was a medical student at the time, told his mother he had something that could help both his dad's pain and his nausea.

"No," she said. "What if the police came to our house and smelled it?"

We asked her how often the police had come to their house and of course she admitted that they never had.

At last we persuaded my Aunt Dorothy to make some brownie mix, then leave the room while my cousin Alex sprinkled some hash over the brownie mix and I stirred the hash into the brownie mix and put it in the oven.

What none of us could have guessed was that this day was the day when the police would, for the very first time, come to their house.

Uncle Nicky ate two of those hash brownies, then fell

asleep. We were sitting in the kitchen, talking quietly, when suddenly we heard a loud bang from the outside door to the bedroom, then somebody shouting. We ran into the bedroom and saw a wild-looking boy of about 15 stretched across the bed with his head in my uncle's lap, crying out over and over again, "Father! Father! I've come home!"

Uncle Nicky, with this beatific hash-induced smile on his face, was stroking the boy's head and murmuring, "There, there."

Well, the three of us just stood there, stunned, and finally Aunt Dorothy asked, "Nicky, is he yours?"

"No, my dear," he said, "I swear I've never seen him before."

So, we were the ones who had to call the police. And they came. By which time my Aunt Dorothy had flushed the hash brownies down the toilet. They took away the boy who had been wandering around Griffith Park for two or three days, high on LSD (this was the 1960s), and who, it turned out, was the son of a doctor my uncle knew slightly.

That week was the last time I ever saw my Uncle Nicky. He died about six months later and he had a huge memorial service with scores of people paying homage to his great humanity.

But, even after death, my Uncle Nicky left his mark. One day, my Aunt Dorothy, cleaning out their garage, noticed some shoeboxes on a shelf. Five of them. When she took them down, she discovered that the first four boxes each contained a pair of Uncle Nicky's elegant shoes, a kind of history of one of his minor vanities, which would have just been perhaps funny and endearing except for what Aunt Dorothy found in the fifth box: $183,000.

Certain this must be some ill-gotten gains, sick with

worry, she called up the Internal Revenue Service and reported what she had found. They came and took away the money. And, by the time they had gone through their months of convoluted calculations, including taxes and penalties, etc., etc., Aunt Dorothy got back something like $10,000 or $12,000.

It was another 50 years before I found out where that money came from. Last summer when my cousin Alex came here for a visit the conversation turned to the shoebox full of cash. "So," I asked my cousin, "what was it? Mafia money?"

He just looked at me and laughed. "Oh, Joyce," he said, "by now surely you could guess that almost anything my dad did would somehow involve women."

I still looked blank.

"Remember back in those early days when it was illegal to perform them?" He gave me a meaningful look.

And then I got it. In more than one way, my Uncle Nicky loved women.

My Aunt Anya

The best thing that ever happened to my father's side of the family was when my Aunt Anya married into it.

It was touch and go for a while as to whether that would actually happen. In his early 30s, my father's older brother, my Uncle Max, became a widower with two young children. In looking around for a second wife, Uncle Max unfortunately became attracted to a very pretty, rather quiet,

19-year-old girl who the rest of the family called "the limp dishrag." In any case, my strong-minded Bubbe had another woman in mind for her son. She was Anya, a 30-year-old daughter of a family friend.

Most women who came of age in the early 1920s were hell-bent on marrying young but not Anya. She'd wanted adventure first, so for several years she'd traveled around the country, marched with her sister suffragettes, become a socialist and then settled for a while in New York City, having been selected to be the very first Jew ever permitted to take nurse's training at the prestigious Bellevue Hospital.

Anya was no beauty. She had rather bulging eyes and, already at 30, a double chin and enough bosom to furnish the prow of a ship. But in spite of that she'd had several flaming love affairs, including one with a famous Greenwich Village painter who, it was said, had been crazy about her for six whole months, though she'd been interested in him for only two. In short, my future Aunt Anya was a *mensch*.

My Uncle Max, on the other hand, was no great bargain. He was such a poor businessman he was about to lose his furniture store. He didn't own his own home and never would. And he was no intellectual heavyweight, to put it mildly. But Anya looked him up and down, found him a little sexy, of sunny disposition, possessing a kind heart, a man who played the fiddle really well and told pretty good jokes. And then, most important of all, there were Uncle Max's two forlorn little boys, aching for a mother.

Oh, talk about dumb luck. Once my Aunt Anya married him, Uncle Max began to realize what a truly worthy man he was. My Aunt Anya had the knack of helping everyone appreciate the great qualities they had never known they possessed. She was not naïve or insincere, she just figured everyone, being human, had to have some good along with the bad. And the good, however small, was what she always emphasized.

Though all my other aunts and uncles were hard-working, solid citizens, they had always rubbed each other the wrong way. Whenever they got together, they argued. When they weren't together, they complained behind each other's backs. Within two or three years, Aunt Anya had changed all that. Almost. They still complained a bit behind each other's backs for the rest of their lives, but when they got together, they at least tried to get along.

Throughout their lives together, 25 years or so, Uncle Max and Aunt Anya remained the financially poorest in my father's family. After my Uncle Max lost his furniture business, he became a rotten insurance salesman. It was my Aunt Anya who uncomplainingly supported the family with her nursing while everyone pretended Uncle Max was supporting it with his few insurance customers.

Every two or three years my parents and I would come from Chicago to visit the rest of the family in Hartford. We always stayed with Aunt Anya and Uncle Max. Aunt Anya would press me into that infinite bosom of hers and lavish me with kisses and superlatives. I wasn't used to kisses and superlatives so I stuck as close to her as possible the whole time I was there in order to store up as much as I could. And, poor or not, my Aunt Anya always threw a great family party for us.

She would welcome each family member at the front door with huge embraces. Uncle Max would play his fiddle; we'd sing along; he'd tell a few jokes; the other uncles would try to top them and all the adults would get a little tight on Manischevitz wine. Every time Aunt Anya would go into the kitchen to check on her stew, some of us kids would follow her. Not for her food – Aunt Anya was no great cook – but for her rich and scary stories about the old country. (She'd come from Czarist Russia when she was 17.)

I remember once when Aunt Anya was telling us this story of how their Christian maid had saved the family store from being smashed to bits by the Cossacks. We were fascinated by how scary those Cossacks were but we were even more mesmerized by the cigarette that dangled from Aunt Anya's mouth which, I think, she had forgotten was there. Her cigarette ash got longer and longer until it finally fell into the stew where it then became part of the stew's delicious taste and aroma. "What did I do?" Aunt Anya asked us. "Did my cigarette ash get in the stew? *Oy, gevalt.* Oh, well, what's done is done. So don't say anything, my dears, because nobody'll be able to tell what I did if you keep quiet." We children didn't tell on Aunt Anya. Instead, we danced around the kitchen with the secret knowledge that, when we finally sat down to eat Aunt Anya's stew, we would be partaking of our very first cigarette!

Though my Uncle Max protested against such a useless waste of money, twice a year Aunt Anya would take their two boys to New York City for a couple of days of museums, plays, ballets, concerts (always up in the second balcony, of course). Though I suppose he enjoyed going to New York, contact with the arts never took hold with my cousin Milton, the older one. He preferred comic books, auto mechanics and, when he grew up, making lots of money owning a liquor store. But Murray, the younger son (whose name my father, originally Meyer, had filched because he liked the sound of it) was ecstatically happy on those trips. Later on young Murray went to the University of Michigan and majored in dance. His first job on Broadway was as a dancer in the show *The Golden Apple.* He danced for a decade, then became a stage manager on and off Broadway. "Mom changed my life from the moment I met her," my cousin lovingly claimed.

Much as my Uncle Max loved my Aunt Anya, he would sometimes get heartburn from her activities. She remained a radical and she wasn't quiet about it. This was the McCarthy era and she would even go so far as to put a notice in the Hartford newspaper, inviting fellow radicals to a book discussion at their house. During those meetings, Uncle Max was so nervous he would stand by the front window of their apartment, on the lookout for the FBI.

But finally, after a number of years, Uncle Max found a way to stop all of Aunt Anya's political activities. He got Alzheimer's at the early age of 52. At first he was his usual gentle self, just a little spacier, but as the disease progressed, he became violent. One day Aunt Anya came home from work to discover he had slashed at one of the radiators with a sledgehammer because it had tried to attack him. It took a while longer but Aunt Anya finally reluctantly put Uncle Max into a veterans' hospital. And there he stayed for the next seven years until he died.

Some time after Uncle Max's death, Aunt Anya moved to New York City near my cousin Murray and she became a haven for many of his theatre friends. I rarely saw her in those years because my life was filled with my two young children and other struggles. But Aunt Anya would often send me her rambling, funny letters, calling me her "Juicy Joycie" and I would feel her warmth flowing through me and out to my two little boys.

One night coming home from a private duty nurse's job (she was 75 at the time), my Aunt Anya was mugged on the Grand Concourse in the Bronx. She spent a month in the hospital, retired from nursing and moved down to Delray Beach, Florida where she bought her first and only home. It was on one of my visits that I finally confessed to Aunt Anya that I had always wished she had been my mother.

Aunt Anya, usually quick to reply, sat and stared at me for nearly a minute. "I never told you this. When you were three years old I tried to adopt you," she said. "Such a sweet, sad little *tsatskaleh* you were. Your father would have been willing but your mother, she had too much pride."

I've never allowed myself to do much speculating about what my life might have been like if that had come to pass. After all, we are what we make of what life hands us.

And sometimes life hands us sorrow upon sorrow. When my Aunt Anya was 87 and my cousin Murray was 59, he told her he had AIDS and they wept in each other's arms. He died six months later and, from that time on, sadness shadowed my Aunt Anya's face.

When she turned 94 Aunt Anya had to move into a nursing home. I would visit her twice a year, watching her ebb away. On my last visit, I wheeled her outdoors to see the flowers and smell some fresh grass. I heard her murmur, "Ech, even the grass here smells like death."

I tried to find a way to lighten her heart a little, knelt down and held her hand. And then she smiled at me.

"Look at you, look at you," she said, "this girl who

somehow made a pretty good life for herself even though I wasn't her mama."

"Oh, no," I said, and I suddenly knew it was true. "Dearest, dearest Anya, you're wrong. You were always there in my head, my dear mama."

My beloved Aunt Anya died when she was 102.

My Father the Writer

New York City, 1927

Shortly after my birth, my father is forced by his father-in-law to accept a package deal: he can spend his days writing his stories instead of supporting his family only if he will also take care of me so my mother can go off to work as a salesgirl at Macy's, at least until my father's stories are written, published and bringing in money.

Every day, after my mother leaves for work, my father

locks me in the bedroom with a book and tells me to be quiet. Even at the age of two, I love books, so that works for the first hour or so. But then I bang on the bedroom door to be let out to go to the bathroom and get more books. My annoyed father slips another book or two through the doorway and tells me to take a nap when I finish reading. But I'm not ready to take a nap; I bang to be let out again. This enrages my father who, one day, pushes me out of our apartment and locks the door.

I am sure he has thrown me out of our family forever and begin to wail with fright and bang on the apartment door. "I be good, Daddy! I be good!" I wail. But there is only silence. After a while, I fall asleep. Two hours later, I wake up on my parents' bed and hear my father speaking to my mother in the next room.

"She's taking a nap. Things went pretty well today. I actually got quite a bit of writing done. Yes, not a bad day at all."

Chicago, 1931

I am six and very sick. My mother and the doctor stand at the foot of my bed. "Do you think she'll recover, doctor?"

"Well, my dear," he says, "it's sometimes difficult to predict with diphtheria." He does not tell her yet that two of his little patients have already died of diphtheria in the last month. Meanwhile, my angry father is pacing back and forth, back and forth. My bedroom by night is actually our dining room and, more to the point, it is also my father's writing room. It has already been 10 days since he has been able to do his writing in his accustomed place and he is fed up.

"For God's sakes," he says, "how much longer is this going

to go on? Where can I find a place to write in some peace and quiet?"

"Oh, Murray," my mother says, "just go into our bedroom and write on the damn bed."

In the evening, when my mother sets out his dinner at the far end of the dining table, he refuses to eat there. Instead, he stands in our tiny Pullman kitchen, plate in hand, and silently shovels in the food. Two more miserable weeks before his writing room returns to normal.

Ravinia, 1933

My mother has arranged our move to a little cottage in a village 30 miles north of Chicago. Now my father has to commute back and forth more than two hours a day, six days a week, to his afternoon and evening job at the Jewish People's Institute. Yet, every morning without fail, he writes for two hours.

One holiday, my father asks my mother to come with him while he visits his new, his only, friend, Rudens. He wants to read Rudens his newest story and get his opinion.

My mother refuses to go. She likes Rudens but she has better things to do.

Glaring, he turns to me. "Put on your coat. You're going with me."

My mother smiles and says just one word to my father, "Coward."

My father storms out of the house and I run after him. We ride in silence for more than an hour, first on the Chicago Northwestern train into downtown Chicago, then the elevated train across the city to the West Side. As we walk the block to Rudens' apartment, my father suddenly says to the air above my head, "She's crazy, you know, his wife. She's been crazy for years. God almighty, Rudens speaks seven languages and can read even more. He might have been a writer himself instead of wasting his time trying to teach English to ignorant immigrants if it wasn't for that damn crazy woman."

My stomach squeezes tight. Rudens has a wife who's crazy? What kind of crazy? Just a little queer-in-the-head crazy like Lily Upjohn who got sleeping sickness years ago and now staggers down the main street of Ravinia, screaming curses at the passersby? Or is Rudens' wife crazy like she'll try to murder us?

"Can we go home now, Daddy?" I whisper.

Once inside Rudens' apartment, my father and Rudens become so immersed in my father's reading of his story, they forget that I am in the room. After about an hour I hear a shuffling sound and, suddenly, she stands there, Rudens' crazy wife, a stocky woman in a shabby black dress, wrinkled stockings and rundown slippers. "It's all right. She just wants to get a look at you," Rudens tells my father.

But she ignores my father. Instead her eyes fix on me. Arms outstretched, she comes toward me, moaning, "*Oy, Zarya! Zarya!*"

As she comes closer I smell her musky flesh and also the lovely smell of sweet violets. One powerful arm lifts me, presses me into her soft breasts. She holds me, dangling, and rocks me back and forth. With the other hand she strokes my face, whispering, "Zarya, *ai zo*, Zarya."

When she presses me so hard I can hardly breathe I call "Daddy!" But Daddy just sits and stares. And then, suddenly, she tears at her dress, bares a breast and tries to press her nipple into my mouth.

"Oh, no, Mona, my dear, no, no!" Rudens pulls me out of her arms, sets me down in a chair and leads her away. When he returns he says, "Please forgive. You see, Zarya, she was the daughter we lost nine years ago."

"Well," my father says, "well, I must admit Rudens, I have been wondering about your wife. Tell me. Why do you do this? Why do you keep her here? For God's sakes, don't you want to be free of her after all this time? She wouldn't even know the difference if you put her in an asylum and you'd be free."

"Oh, my friend," replies Rudens, looking at my father as though seeing him for the first time. "You don't understand. For years she was the one who kept me from despair. I will never abandon her. Never."

My father shrugs. "Suit yourself." Then he picks up his manuscript and holds it aloft. "So. Tell me what you think, Rudens. Doesn't my new story have great depth and power?"

This story will eventually appear in *Esquire*. Then, six months later, *Esquire* prints another. Almost a year after that, *Scribner's* accepts his novella. There is talk about how my father and another Chicago writer, Nelson Algren, may be two of the most promising young writers of the American Midwest.

One of my mother's friends throws a big party for my famous father. While my father refuses to read aloud one of his stories to his enraptured audience, he does agree to pose in front of his hostess' fireplace, one arm carefully placed on the mantel, and sing the Russian song *"Ochichorniya"* in his rich baritone voice. He knows he sings well. Opera singers told him he might have had a career if he hadn't chosen to be a writer instead. My mother's friends all envy my mother because not only is my father a true artist, in contrast to their own dull, though rich, businessmen husbands, but he even dramatically looks the part: darkly handsome with smoldering, hooded eyes and the mysterious air of the poet. They are all in love with him.

My father, on the other hand, is in love with Walt Whitman. "Whitman's like Beethoven," my father tells me. "They both pushed boundaries." About once a month my father instructs me to sit on the living room couch, then strikes a pose across the room from me and recites verse after verse of Whitman's "Song of Myself."

"I celebrate myself and sing myself / And what I assume you shall assume." When he finishes the whole poem he says, "Not bad, huh? Your old dad knows how to put across a poem, eh?"

I always answer the same way. "Yes, Daddy."

One summer, Whitman's great "Song of the Open Road" so inspires my father that he decides to take leave from his job for a whole month to wander across this great nation. Unlike the earlier trip to New Orleans, my mother and I are left at home as my father sets off to thumb rides, hop freight trains and continue his search for Whitman's Heart of America.

Yet, though he encounters factory workers, housewives, farmers and hoboes, he returns in only 10 days, bringing back no stories.

"What happened?" my mother asks.

"Nothing much," replies my father.

"Oh, nothing much? Too much for you, you mean," my

mother says.

He stops reciting Whitman and turns instead to Beethoven, whose powerful symphonies fill our house.

Then, for one year, two years, three long years, my father receives nothing but rejection slips. His mouth droops, his eyes are more hooded than ever, he scowls when he looks at me and my mother. At mealtimes, we sit at the table, each of us with a book propped up behind our plate, silently reading. There are times, for as long as two weeks, when my father is completely silent.

Yet, year after year, my father sits in his big armchair in my parents' bedroom and writes. Lack of persistence is not his shortcoming.

Lake Michigan, 1937

My mother and I tiptoe around the house because the bedroom door must be kept open. My father suffers more and more from claustrophobia. But, on this early November day, my father does something unusual: he leaves his bedroom chair after writing for only 20 minutes, stands at the doorway, and asks me to go for a walk with him. I am 12 years old; he has never asked me to do this before.

We are alone as we walk the two blocks eastward toward the high bluffs overlooking Lake Michigan. It is an unusual time of year for us to be taking this walk. The trees are bare, the sky gray. Maybe it will snow today. I try to walk beside my father, skipping to keep up. But his steps grow longer, so he is always two or three paces ahead of me. He never turns to look back at me.

As we pass some woods, I tell him, "Daddy, you know

what? Last summer, when I was going by here, something suddenly let out this huge scream that made me so scared and you know what it was? It was a giant parrot! Just sitting over there, like it was South America or something! And it couldn't fly away because it had this long chain around its leg. Isn't that amazing?" My father glances at the woods, half-alarmed, as though to check the truth of my story but there is no parrot there today.

When we reach the edge of the bluff, he abruptly stops, then for the first time drops behind me. The high rocky cliff makes me dizzy as it plunges almost straight down to the beach. My father is so close I can feel the heat of his sturdy body. Why is he so close? Why are we here? Does he, does he . . .

Yes, now I know why this walk seems so strange. He might push me over the edge and get rid of me forever to make his life better. My heart begins to thump, thump so loudly I wonder if he can hear it. Then he brushes against me. "No!" I cry, fall to the ground and frantically crawl away from the edge. My father stares at me, astonished. "I, I have a stone in my shoe," I tell him, my voice shaking, then sit up and begin to untie my shoe.

My father takes a step toward me, his arm raised, then shrugs and says, "Well, whatever," and starts down the long, steep, rickety stairway to the beach.

As I descend after him, I imagine falling, rolling down faster and faster, hitting my father, the two of us hurtling to the bottom. But we reach the bottom without incident. Then we walk in silence along the deserted beach. The gray, crashing, indifferent waves inch higher and higher up the sand. Is this where it will happen instead? Which moment will it be when he pushes me into that cold, thick water? After half an hour, we turn and head home. No word is spoken by either of us until we enter our house, when my father says to me, "I'm behind in my writing," goes into his bedroom and, for the first time in years, closes the door.

I climb the stairs to my attic room and lie down on my bed. Through the window the bare branches of the huge oak tree look as familiar and as menacing as my father's arms.

Washington, DC, 1947

After World War II, my father goes to Italy to help relocate Jewish refugees. While there he somehow saves a bit of money. His brothers and sisters whisper that he's acquired it illegally on the Italian black market. In any case, when he returns to America, my father invests most of it in the stock market, lives frugally and never has to work again. By the time he is 60, he is a millionaire, has married his landlady and bought a big apartment overlooking the Golden Gate Bridge. Unfortunately, even with money worries out of the way, he is never able to recapture his early promise as a writer. As for his leftism, before his mind is ultimately lost to the haze we call Alzheimer's, my father has voted twice for Ronald Reagan.

Shortly after his third wife dies, my father comes East on a rare visit. The purpose of his trip gradually dawns on the rest of us in the family: it is to determine whom – his sister Beatrice; his sister-in-law Ruth, widow of his younger brother Bernie; or me, his daughter – he will choose to take care of him for the rest of his life.

First, my father goes to Hartford, Connecticut to visit

his sister, my Aunt Beatrice. Aunt Beatie has a reputation as a fine cook and has always been a sweet, sweet lady, so we figure there is a good chance she might be The One. "Oh, I've been baking up a storm," Aunt Beatrice tells me in a phone call. "After all these years, I'm so looking forward to seeing your dad."

Not for long. By the second day, my father has let my Aunt Beatrice know that she uses an unhealthy amount of butter in her cooking and talks too much. He puts in a call to his sister-in-law, Ruth. "Pick me up today, will you?" he asks. "My stomach can't take any more of this." After Aunt Ruth arrives, flustered Aunt Beatie says to my father, "Oh, dear, I am so sorry if I did anything wrong."

My father nods grimly, offering only one word of farewell. "So." Then he turns his back and gets into Aunt Ruth's Cadillac.

A day and a half later, my Aunt Ruth, a tough, no-nonsense kind of lady who ran my Uncle Bernie's sporting goods business for 40 years, calls me. "Let me tell you," she says, "I've already had quite enough of your dad. Do you know what he's had the gall to tell me? That my house is pretentious, that playing golf is a waste of time and mahjong is even stupider, and that my friends are empty-headed bores. Well, I'm telling you – he's taking the plane for Washington tomorrow and you need to be there to pick him up."

At Dulles the next day, I watch my father's lurching gait as he comes toward me.

"You're looking old. Not eating right, I'll bet," he says by way of greeting.

"Welcome," I reply. I have to at least try to make it work. "How was Hartford?"

"Those aunts of yours. Let me tell you. They're nothing to write home about."

Back at my house, I serve dinner to my father and my husband, Richard. "You people eat a little better than your aunts do," my father informs us. "You ought to eat some raw peanuts the way I do. Good for cleansing the whole system. People are amazed by my endurance."

Five months after his visit, my father calls from his home in San Francisco. "Well, I've decided who I'll be living with," he tells me. "You can pass it on to your aunts. His name is Aristotle. He is a used book dealer of only the best books and he's a Harvard graduate, no less. Looked over my books and said I had a fine collection. Seems quite intelligent. More my type than the family."

For the next three years, I talk on the phone with my father once or twice each year. Only once do I hear from Mr. Aristotle – a year after I have last heard from my father. He is calling to say that my father wants no more connection with his family.

Then – silence. My father has Alzheimer's and can no longer talk.

One day, a formal letter comes from a lawyer informing me of my father's death.

Rappahannock, 2017

For decades, I am convinced that I could never be a writer. Though I admire good writing and am an avid reader, writing seems like a self-centered pursuit that inevitably circumscribes everything else. Writing is at odds with living life. My father made that much clear.

I am in my 60s when I first write a piece about my life for a course I'm taking. To me, it doesn't seem so hot, but the other students like it. After that, the more I write, the easier each story feels.

So I keep going.

Sophie and Sarah

I spent some of the happiest times of my childhood with my grandmothers: my mother's mother, Sophie, and my father's mother, Sarah. It wasn't until I was in my 20s that I learned why neither of my parents liked their mothers.

I was 22 and had gone to live and work for a year in Los Angeles, the same city where my grandmother Sophie and my two aunts, Dorothy and Violet, lived. Grandma Sophie had asked me to stay with her. We had a great time together: she baking me and my boyfriend her superb apple pies; me keeping her from being lonely. Some evenings she'd have me read novels to her because her eyesight was getting bad. Once, she chose Norman Mailer's *The Naked and the Dead* for me to read to her. I remember coming across the first occurrence of Mailer's version of the "f-word" – frigging – and wildly asking myself how I could possibly say that terrible word to my sweet, delicate grandma.

I saw no way around it without betraying the author, so I steeled myself and said it. And said it again, every time it appeared. It wasn't until the third day of my reading, my having repeated this word dozens of times, that Grandma Sophie finally asked, "What does that word 'frigging' mean, dear?"

I had my answer ready. "It means 'darn,' Grandma."

"What an odd way of saying it," she said.

But then one day, for the very first time, I saw a quite different Grandma Sophie. It was the day when we learned that my 12-year-old cousin Arthur, Dorothy and Nicky's son, was still wetting his bed.

"Disgusting," she said, and her voice no longer sounded sweet. "He's doing it deliberately and if I were Dorothy I'd beat him until he stopped."

"Grandma!" I said. "Arthur can't help it."

"Oh, yes he can," she said. "And besides, you know you can't trust a boy who won't look you in the eye. If he isn't stopped now he'll always be trouble."

The next day I happened to mention to my Aunt Violet what Grandma Sophie had said. She gave me a curious look and then asked, "Haven't you ever wondered why your mother is such a cold woman?"

"What do you mean?"

"Well," Aunt Violet said, "I had a part in it too, a shameful part. The only way I can excuse myself is by saying I was just a kid then. And so was your Aunt Dorothy."

It seems my grandfather doted on my mother when she was a little girl. And she, in turn, adored him. Because he was a famous foreign correspondent and also because he kept a well-known opera singer as his mistress, my grandfather was away from home a lot. But when he'd come home, he'd bring my mother exotic gifts, like the little ermine coat, hat and muff he'd had made for her in Russia. And being himself a daring man, he was much more delighted by my mother's daring and free spirit than my grandmother's conventional ways. But it was my mother's daring one night that apparently began the lopsided, unholy war between mother and child.

My grandpa and grandma had put on a big party for Grandpa's friend, the renowned Russian basso opera singer Fyodor Chaliapin who was about to perform at the Met. At the party, Chaliapin sang a few Russian songs for the other guests. Of course, he had a beautiful, powerful voice. While he was singing, my mother climbed out of her bed and, dressed in her Doctor Denton pajamas, came padding into the living room and went and sat on my grandpa's lap.

After Chaliapin had finished singing, my little mother piped up, "I can sing too."

My grandfather laughed and said, "Sing for the great Chaliapin, my child."

So she did. She sang, "I never saw a purple cow; I never hope to see one. But I can tell you anyhow, I'd rather see than be one!"

Well, Chaliapin roared with laughter. He swept my mother up into his arms and sang her a sweet little Russian lullaby.

But my grandmother Sophie didn't laugh, oh no. From then on, she began to find ways to curb her out-of-control daughter. As my mother refused to be controlled, my grandmother made the discipline harsher. Whenever my grandfather was away from home, Grandma Sophie would lock my mother into her bedroom all day long. Tell her what a bad child she was. Shun her and make my two aunts and all the servants shun her too. But it was when they moved to their summer place in the Berkshires that the worst began.

My mother was totally alone out there, ignored by everyone, except when my grandfather would come home. Those times she would run to him for comfort but was afraid to tell him what was happening to her. And then he'd soon be gone again.

But then came the day when my grandfather came home and my mother did not joyfully run into his arms. She just stood there and scowled, angry at him for not rescuing her from my grandmother. But since he knew nothing about it, he just stared at her, puzzled and hurt, went into his study and closed the door.

Then one day, after my grandfather was gone again, my grandmother sent my aunts Dorothy and Violet to shadow my mother. They discovered her up in the loft of the barn. She had this raggedy, ugly little dog in her arms and was rocking it and humming to it and feeding it with some food she must have stolen from the kitchen.

Aunt Violet told me, "Of course we ran and reported it to Mama. And Mama marched to the barn, took the dog and drowned it in a pail. Your mother stayed in that barn for a day and a night."

But over the next two or three years, my mother was so lonely she'd try harder than ever to hide and nurse all kinds of animals, including wild ones. Whenever my two aunts ratted on her, my grandmother saw to it that each of those strays was killed.

"At first Mama had drowned the animals herself," Aunt Violet told me. "But then came a terrible day when she made your mother drown them. Your mother begged Mama not to make her. She cried terribly, wailing these big gulping wails until Dorothy and I put our hands over our ears and ran away."

And, suddenly, as my Aunt Violet was telling me this, I remembered a day when I was seven years old. There was an old alley cat that used to hang around our house and one day she gave birth to five tiny kittens. My mother drowned them all. I cried and begged her not to drown the little white one, not that one. But she drowned that one too. I couldn't bear to watch her hands. And her face, her face had turned to stone.

Perhaps it's no wonder she had so very little interest in nurturing by the time I came along.

‹›

I was in my late 20s when I went to visit my tough old Bubbe in an old folks' home. I hadn't seen her in years. My father's youngest sister, Aunt Beatie, took me there, and it was on the way that I asked her a question I'd been waiting to ask. As I was asking it, I could feel something heavy sitting in the pit of my stomach and I knew it was fear of her answer. Would my father's story be as terrible as my mother's? He certainly showed no more enthusiasm or capacity for parenting than she did.

"Why does my father hate Bubbe so much?" I asked. "Did she beat him when he was a kid or what?"

"Oh," said Aunt Beatie, "yeah, she'd slap the six of us around if we didn't work hard enough. But she was an equal opportunity slapper so we all got over it, except your dad. He resented it terribly. Actually, he got slapped the least but I'll admit he was worked the hardest of any of us because he was the strongest. But we always knew our parents were basically good people, just poor and struggling.

"Actually I think your Bubbe was more proud of your dad than of the rest of us because he was so smart but he was forever being sulky toward her. And when he went off to college, the only one of us ever to go to college, she'd even send him some of her hard-earned egg money and he never once thanked her. But you know what I think might have made him angriest of all toward her? He was ashamed, ashamed that a mother of his was illiterate – he who was going to be a famous writer someday had a mother who wouldn't learn to read. Let me tell you, learning to read was never high on your Bubbe's agenda. Her agenda was just sheer survival for all of us. And, hey, I think we all wound up pretty okay.

"But I'll bet you didn't know this," said Aunt Beatie, laughing. "You were her favorite of all. Remember that year you lived with Bubbe and Zayde? Remember how Bubbe once rescued you from one of the boarders, that old pederast, Mr. Kaminsky? He'd backed you into the dark pantry and tried to take your panties down? When Bubbe discovered what was going on she grabbed Mr. Kaminsky by the collar and yanked him away from you, hollering so loudly everyone ran to see who'd gotten killed."

"I remember just a little," I said.

"Ah, well, what you don't know," said Aunt Beatie, "was that when Bubbe ordered that family out of the house, she and Zayde lost part of their income that year. Let me tell you, never, never had Bubbe ever done anything like that before. Money was her priority because there was always so little of it. But you, well, she thought you were special."

It had been many years since I'd seen Bubbe. She was now 91 but she looked almost the same. She grabbed my face, then gave me big smacking kisses, over and over, on both cheeks. A torrent of Yiddish poured over my head.

"What's she saying?" I asked Aunt Beatie.

"She says she remembers you on the farm when you were like a little bird, never still, chirping and hopping everywhere you went. She'd sometimes stop her work to watch you out the window. And she says she knew, she knew you loved Zayde more than you loved her. Everyone did. But she'll never forget one marvelous day when you came running into the house with a fistful of little yellow flowers – must have been buttercups or maybe even dandelions – and you gave them to her and you told her: 'I love you, Bubbe,' and then you kissed her on her nose and you ran out again. No, she never forgot that."

As Bubbe was telling us this, tears began to stream down her face. "Oh, my God," Aunt Beatie said. "I've never seen Mother cry before, not when baby Jacob died, not even when your Zayde died."

Bubbe kept swaying back and forth, saying *"oy, oy, oy"* so

I leaned over and I kissed her on her nose. She laughed and gave me a little slap.

We said goodbye; she squeezed my hands. She was still so strong, my hands ached for minutes afterwards. And I never saw her again.

Looking back, I wonder what dark forces, beyond just simple jealousy, made my seemingly sweet grandmother Sophie feel no pity toward my innocent mother.

But my father, on the other hand – well, Aunt Beatie's story had not made me feel any kinder toward him. Perhaps it was exactly because I was his child, he who had rejected her as though she was less than human, that my grandmother felt my little bunch of flowers meant so much. I think it meant that I, daughter of her ungrateful son, felt she was lovable. If I had always given her less love than for my grandfather . . . well, it was still love, and she took every little bit of love and then carried on with life.

And I realize now that in her unique way, she was grateful and could love me back because there was still, and there had always been, a soft little place hidden in her tough old heart.

My Mother the Spy

Though my father was the first to re-marry and it took many years before my mother did, it was she who orchestrated their separation and divorce when I was 15. She had realized that times had changed and she now had the chance and ability to do something far more interesting than selling clothes at Macy's. She had even done some duty as a spy for the Jewish Anti-Defamation League, posing, with her Nordic looks as "Hilda Holland" and joining the German-American Bund of Milwaukee, where she helped to gather information to discredit the anti-Semitic propaganda about the Protocols of the Elders of Zion and other anti-Jewish garbage. This specious screed had infected the country with a belief in a worldwide Jewish conspiracy in the late 1930s, though a definitive refutation was published by her father, Herman Bernstein. If neither she nor anyone else was able to do much to stem the tide of anti-Jewish sentiment, which persisted and flourished even after World War II, she at least proved she could work effectively outside the home.

Convinced that she could get a good job and support herself and me, she was done with my father for good. My father could see this coming but, since change was what he hated and feared the most, he clung to the last strands of their marriage, listening to my mother's bitter, biting analysis of him until my mother just savagely cut the strands into little bits and we moved.

She and I moved from Winnetka (a town near Ravinia) into an apartment on the north side of Chicago, where she took a position as head of a housing agency. I went to the nearby Waller High School for my last three years. My mother and I shared housework at our new apartment. I did the cleaning, the marketing and cooking of our meals during the week. My mother would cook on the weekends and sometimes invite friends over. She had a few lovers but each had a set of weaknesses that she found contemptible. She was rather like Gertrude Stein, about whom it was said that she idealized friendships and invariably ended up destroying them.

After about six months, my mother fell in love with a 27-year-old painter. He was a fine painter, a self-contained young man, unlike anyone she'd ever known before. She began to half-live with him (he had told her he had no intention of living with her full-time) and half-live with me. Our apartment, now without an adult much of the time, began to be the place where the neighborhood kids, most of them Irish Catholics, came to smoke cigarettes, drink weak beer and make out. They were older than I was – nice kids but ready to be adults. I wasn't so ready, but deeply wanted them to like me, so got myself into a slightly scary scenario where I was constantly worried about whether the police would come to round up the kids who hadn't gone home when their parents expected them to.

One day my mother didn't call me and didn't come home, nor did she come the next day, or the next. I frantically called her friends, sure that she'd had some kind of accident. All of them told me not to worry, but wouldn't tell me anything more. Finally, someone told me my mother was in the hospital with a stomach ailment.

The truth, which I discovered days later, was that she had tried to commit suicide because her young painter-lover had told her he didn't love her. When she returned she was very quiet, visibly sad.

I finished high school and went off to Berkeley. My mother got a better job and another lover. Then she moved to Washington DC, got a better job and an older lover, the chair of the board she was working for. That one lasted about six months.

When she was 43 she met Joe Cloud, the handsome, debonair, hard-drinking, womanizing Metro editor of the

Washington Post, and married him. At the age of 44, she had a son by him. The day she came home from the hospital she found him in their bed with another woman.

By this time my mother was disillusioned not only about men but also about Communism, horrified by the rumors of Stalin's purges and what she saw as his betrayal of what might have been the world's greatest hope for the brotherhood of mankind. Nonetheless, she remained a passionate leftist. After the McCarthy era in the '50s, she became an expatriate, living abroad for almost 20 years.

She lived in Guanajuato, Mexico, then France, Australia, New Zealand and back to Europe. During those latter years, she drove an old Volkswagen microbus from one campground to another, usually in northern Europe in the summertime and in southern Europe in winter. After a few years of this, she became famous among campers in some parts of the continent, this little old self-sufficient woman with her wild white hair who was sharp as a tack about politics, literature and just about any other subject you might discuss with her. But when some fellow camper, perhaps delighted after an evening's talk, would invite her to come visit his home someday, she would always answer, "Oh, I don't expect to ever see you again. I find long-term friendships disappointing."

She came back to the US in the mid-70s and became the head of the Grey Panthers in San Francisco. In a few weeks, she had found a way to help the elderly. First, she managed to get interviewed by the San Francisco newspapers, claiming that American banks were cheating the elderly by charging them for their savings accounts. That led to her being invited to Washington DC to testify before a Senate subcommittee about this subject. She stayed with me and my second husband, Richard.

After her interview with *PBS News Hour,* I took her to the airport. "Well," she said as we walked through the terminal, "I see that all you could get was a man in a wheelchair."

For the first time in my life I spat my words at her in a rage, "He's worth a hundred of you!" I told her.

And, for the first time in my life, I saw shock and a tiny bit of fear on my mother's face.

I knew I had told her the truth. And I think in some way, she knew it too.

A few weeks later the Senate passed a bill requiring banks to allow all people 60 and over to have free savings accounts. She wrote me several pleasant letters which I answered pleasantly but with no hurry. After a few months, her letters began to contain little digs, then larger ones. I stopped writing to her and never saw or wrote to her again. A few years later she died of a heart attack in San Francisco when she was 80, then living in a low-income housing project for seniors.

When she died, I'd imagined that, because of her prickly character, there would be very few people at her memorial service. I was wrong. My half-brother told me that there were more than 100 in that community hall, most of them poor people like herself. One by one they rose to tell the others how my mother had fought government and private agencies to help them get medical services, food stamps, jobs.

Of my two parents, I must say I admired my mother far more than my father. He was one of the most self-centered, childish human beings I have ever known. She, on the other hand, was always a complex woman who was interested in other people, in both positive and destructive ways, though there lurked times when her acerbic mouth and contemptuous manner bit and enraged me and others.

But in the months after her death, I would often think back on how hard my mother's life had been, from her childhood when she had had only sporadic love from one person, her father, to her sterile marriages and love affairs and then to her brave leap off into a totally new life in late middle age. And she never stopped trying, I think, to be her father's girl, ending her remarkable old age by making a small but good national change for the elderly, and lastly, how resilient she remained unto death.

She was not a loving mother but she kept me alive and physically well.

During her 20s and 30s, she had had five abortions and I am grateful I was not one of them.

Jean and Pierre

The year was 1951 and I was 26 years old – a curvy little redhead, living on a tiny farm in Clarksville, Maryland, teaching at a boarding school and driving back and forth in the only car I could afford to buy, a 1932 Model B Ford.

Next door to me was a large, beautiful farm owned by two French foreign correspondents who worked for Agence France Presse, the French version of the Associated Press.

One day I knocked on their door and asked if they would allow me to take walks on their land. They said of course, invited me in for coffee and then showed me all around their farm.

I liked them both: Pierre Roland, in his late 20s, stocky, full of fun, loved farming, was married. The other was Jean Davidson, intellectual, handsome, kind, thoughtful and single – too old for me at 37, I was sure. But when he called one day to invite me to a party, we discovered we had a funny little family connection. His father, a famous sculptor of the early 20th century, had once created a bust of my illustrious grandfather. Somehow that was the first step in drawing us together, making us feel it was meant to be.

What really impressed me about Jean wasn't just that he was a worldly foreign correspondent, but that he was also a racing car driver who often competed on European and American tracks. That gave him the delicious aura of a dashing daredevil and I lo-oved dangerous men. So when Jean asked me, a month later, if I would become his girlfriend, I immediately said yes.

I have to give credit to both Jean and Pierre for helping me become more sophisticated that year I was their next-door neighbor. They taught me by example how to drink and smoke as though I weren't merely standing around self-consciously drinking and smoking but was quite intelligently discussing the fate of the world while incidentally standing around drinking and smoking.

Pierre enjoyed instructing me about the strengths and weaknesses of various breeds of cows, sheep and chickens, at times leaping casually from chickens to world leaders – each being for him of apparently equal importance. From Jean, I became adept at distinguishing one racing car from another but more importantly, for the first time in my life, I began to appreciate modern art, of which he knew a great deal. Frenchmen, racing cars, chickens, world leaders, modern art, a sophisicated love affair . . . 1951 was a heady year for me.

However, I was about to pay a price for the friendship of those lovely Frenchmen. In spite of their good will, in spite of their great kindnesses to me, they each brought me close to sudden and violent death.

The first time was when Jean had me drive his Maserati, his beautiful blue racing car. I loved riding in it but God knows why he ever, for a single minute, trusted me to drive it. He knew I had driven only two cars in my whole life – my 1932 Ford and, before that, a scruffy 1936 Dodge coupe that had fallen apart one evening on a traffic-jammed San Francisco hill.

A few months after I'd gotten to know him, Jean told me he needed to go to Paris for two weeks. Would I drive his Maserati back from the airport?

Of course I told him no way.

"Oh, my dear," he assured me, "have no fear. She's much, much easier to drive than your Ford. Your Ford is like a grumpy old grandmama. My Maserati is more like an elegant mistress who's willing to show you how to dance with grace and ease."

I reluctantly agreed but insisted he first give me a lesson or two. Perhaps, I thought, I would be good at it. I would be like some minor movie star, wearing a beautiful silken scarf and dark glasses, whipping down the road in that gorgeous, sleek piece of danger. Unfortunately, the day came for Jean to leave and we had somehow never found the time to practice.

Jean drove the two of us to the national airport as I desperately tried to pay attention to how he used the pedals and gear shift. He got out of the car, handed me the keys and, by way of a complete set of instructions, told me, "You need to remember only two things, my dear. First, she runs so smoothly she will almost drive herself. And second, she will sometimes try to surprise you, so do pay attention."

We kissed and I watched him disappear into the terminal. Then I slipped into the driver's seat for the first time. My heart thumped loudly but who can hear a frightened heart when a self-assured racing car is whizzing you out of the airport? Half an hour later, out in the Maryland country-side, I finally relaxed a little. Driving a racing car truly is a beautiful experience, so fluid that, as the driver, you feel as though you and the car are a single being, gliding smoothly, powerfully, with perfection, down the road. And that's how it was, for a while.

Until (and I swear I never saw a single warning sign) I suddenly came to the end of the road I'd been driving on and had to either make an abrupt left turn or plow into a grove of trees. Those trees were coming at me so fast it suddenly dawned on me that this powerful car had just been waiting for the perfect moment to show me its great surprise, the one that Jean had warned me about. And when I glanced down at the speedometer, it told me I was going not the 60 miles per hour I thought, but 92. Racing cars are sneaky that way.

It was the first time in my life I really, truly knew I could die. Please, please, not yet, I thought.

I spun that Maserati around I don't know how many times trying to make that turn, narrowly missing two stop signs, several ditches and tree after tree after tree before I finally landed by the side of the road, turned off the engine and hyperventilated for about 15 minutes. During those 15 minutes, not a single car and only one truck came by and I remember staring at the old farmer obliviously driving past me and thinking, "Oh, mister, you don't know how lucky you are! I just saved you from having to look at my bloody, mangled body!" And then, finally, that innocent Maserati and I crept the rest of the way home.

So much for loving danger. I never told Jean what had nearly happened to his Maserati, but that near-death experience sparked a great love of life in me.

The second time I almost died, Jean's friend the artist Alexander Calder saw it happen, and played an odd role in the aftermath of the incident.

Jean had known Sandy Calder for many years and he loved Calder's work so much he had filled the living room in their farmhouse with Calder mobiles and stabiles and circus figures and paintings and chess sets and God knows what else.

About three months after I'd first gotten to know my French neighbors, Sandy, his wife Louisa and their two young daughters came for a visit. I wasn't sure what to make of Sandy: he looked like a sloppy teddy bear. He liked his food, and he loved his drink. He often behaved like a mischievous clown and it seemed as though both his nimble brain and clever fingers had these spurts of creativity and energy. If nothing else was available, he'd make newspaper airplanes and flick them at us. Of course, they were uniquely Calderish paper airplanes. Oh, I wish I had saved one. Louisa Calder looked a bit like a gypsy queen, vibrant with color and wild jewelry, some of which had been fashioned out of coffee cans by Sandy.

The Calders began coming to visit every six weeks or so. It was on perhaps their third visit, sometime in the fall, that we decided to celebrate Louisa Calder's birthday. I'm not even sure it was her birthday. It could very well have just been Sandy's excuse for a party. On the day of the celebration, we ate our midday meal on the patio, imbibed plenty of wine and then everyone retired to take naps, except for me. I chose to take a stroll instead.

It was a beautiful day. I wandered through Jean's and Pierre's woods for a while, picked some wildflowers and then ambled across the pasture below their house. By this time I was getting a bit tired, so I lay down in a little hollow in the middle of the pasture with my head resting against a small boulder and fell asleep.

I was awakened by a shot. The bullet had come so close to my right ear that it made that ear deaf for several minutes. I got to my feet and there, about 50 yards from me, stood Pierre, holding his rifle.

We stared at each other for a moment. I'll admit, I did kind of expect Pierre to come running frantically to see how I was, having just nearly blown off my head. Instead, he just stood there, rigid, holding tight to his rifle as though it was his protector instead of his near-destroyer.

As the seconds went by and he didn't move, I finally walked across the pasture to him. I could see he was in some kind of a daze. I reached my arms around him and hugged and rocked him as though he were my little boy, though he was nearly twice my size.

His first words stunned me. "Please, please, Joyce, don't tell anyone I almost killed you. Oh, God, I'd never live it down."

Hey, my friend, I thought, you almost killed me and all you can do is ask me not to tattle on you? But I really couldn't be angry with him – he was so wildly distraught. "I thought you were a fox," he said. "With your red hair, I thought I was shooting a fox. They've been killing our chickens." He wept and wept and then, at long last, said, "Oh, please forgive me. How on earth could I have been so careless?"

A bit to my own astonishment, out of my mouth popped the words, "Pierre, I promise you I'll never tell anyone what happened." As soon as I said that, I wanted to take it back. Really, I could hardly wait to tell the whole world about what had happened.

Finally, we walked back to the house and we each had a martini to calm ourselves. When all the others, except for Sandy, came down from their naps, we chatted and I could see Pierre beginning to relax.

Then Sandy Calder lumbered down the stairs, made himself a drink, turned and said, "Hey, Pierre, aren't you happy you didn't kill Joyce? Or are ya kinda peeved cause ya couldn't quite pull it off?"

Pierre turned pale as Sandy continued. "Oh, I gotta tell ya, pal, at first I wondered, maybe I'm having some kind of goofy nightmare. But then I thought, nah . . . " As he nattered on, it looked like my near-killer was about to pass out.

So, the cat was out of the bag. We each told our story of what had happened. Louisa rushed to hug us both. Jean said to Pierre, "Perhaps no more rifle shooting, *mon ami?*"

Pierre's wife sneered at him. "So stupid," she said.

At the time, I thought Sandy was kind of cruel and cold-hearted but later I realized that he perhaps set us free. We all remained friends. The Calders continued to visit every six weeks or so. Pierre's wife went on an extended visit to Paris and nobody missed her.

I moved away from Clarksville before the Frenchmen did. I got a job in DC at an ad agency working on the All-American Cowboy, Pick Temple's, children's TV show for our client, Giant Foods. After Pierre's wife left him, he moved back to Paris and a year later remarried. He assured me his new wife was such a sweetheart that, after he'd told her how he had almost killed me, she laughed and gave him a big kiss.

After Jean moved back to Paris, he would send me cards and letters from the many places he was covering for stories for Agence France Presse. When I told him on one of his visits to me that I had met my future husband, he said, "Ah, you know, I once thought perhaps you and I . . . " And left his words dangling there. The next year we stopped writing and we never saw each other again.

About five years ago, I happened to pick up a book about Alexander Calder at a friend's house and there was a photo of my ex-boyfriend Jean Davidson living in France with his wife. He had married Sandy Calder's daughter.

Who Knew?

Without dwelling too much on the details, let it be said that my late first husband, an alcoholic newspaperman and photographer, was not the love of my life. The Albanian guardsman Rassim and the young Michigan athlete Jimmy Wonnell had set the standard, but the real McCoy was yet to come.

If anyone had told me early on that actually the love

of my life was an upright young man now living in New Hampshire, who attended the Congregational church every Sunday, played on the lacrosse and ice hockey teams at the state university, had not yet read a single piece of European literature and intended to be, of all things, an apple farmer – all I can say is, thank God I didn't find him until I was 45 and he was 48.

Sometime in my early 40s, longing to become a minor Margaret Mead (or even a major Margaret Mead), I went back to school to get a master's in cultural anthropology. By this time, my first marriage was on its last leg. Midway through grad school, I had to take over the full support of my children. I changed course to become a high school teacher, took a bunch of those awful education classes and then, rather late in the game, began wondering where in this world I could teach something like high school anthropology.

We were strangers the day I called Richard Abell, a social studies professor at Montgomery County High who had begun a program in anthropology for his students, to ask if he might be willing to take me on as his student teacher. His answer was "no." A nice no, but no.

That might have been it right there.

∽

Richard was raised in a pacifist Congregational community where people believed the commandment "Thou shalt not kill" was meant to be taken seriously. So, when he turned 21 and came before his draft board during World War II, he declared himself a conscientious objector and asked to be assigned to the medical corps to drive an ambulance.

Well, instead of ambulance driving, he was sent first to Oregon to fight forest fires and then, perhaps due to his training in horticulture, to Ohio to work in a plant pathology lab. And, it was there in Ohio that one day taking a shower in his dorm, Richard was suddenly struck by a terrible, terrible headache, then found he could hardly breathe or stand up.

He had caught a serious case of polio, making his legs forever useless. Though for several weeks it was almost impossible for him to breathe without living in an iron lung, his doctors and nurses were eventually able to teach him to use a new set of his remaining chest muscles. He also had to strengthen his shoulder and back muscles so he could raise his right arm with the help of his left hand and arm. Even after he got out of the iron lung, he was in the hospital for months.

Gradually, he who had gloried in the power of his youth and his agility now discovered his new strengths lay instead in patience and determination. So he left behind his dream of becoming an apple farmer, went back to the University of New Hampshire, painfully climbed up and down stairs to his classes on leg braces and crutches and finally received his master's in history and education.

Only one school of the dozen he applied to in the late 1940s was willing to take the risk of hiring a polio cripple in a wheelchair. That school was Sidwell Friends. (When the Obama girls attended this school, it was partly because, back sometime in the 1950s, Richard had persuaded the headmaster of Sidwell to begin the long, long process of opening up that school to black students.) By the time I met him in the 1970s, he was a great and renowned teacher, now working in the Montgomery County Public Schools because he had a family to support and that school system paid much better than Sidwell.

Back to our fateful phone call. Fortunately, I did not take no for answer. After 20 minutes of my showing him what an intelligent person I was – actually, his kind of intelligent person – he said, "You know? I think I will take you on as my student teacher after all."

Unfortunately, once I got into the classroom, things did not go smoothly. I had by now forgotten what it was like to be a teenager and those education courses I'd taken were of no help at all. So, on my first day of student teaching, I delivered part of my graduate seminar talk on the cultural and societal aspects of dwellings around the world. Igloos! Yurts! Mud huts!

Their response was basically, up yours, lady.

On the other hand, they loved Richard. He was quietly disciplined and deliberate, in that famously New England way, yet at the same time daring and innovative. This was the early 70s, when schools were open to innovation. For example, he'd invented an urban studies class that kids vied to get into. He would train them and then send them out in teams: one team, say, to research and volunteer at DC's decrepit St. Elizabeth's mental institution, another to discover all the problems there were in starting up the then-new area metro system, a third to do a poll of people who were being dispossessed by the redevelopment project that had begun ripping apart southwest DC. On weekends, Richard would take his archaeology students on digs in various parts of Maryland. And, when his high school seemed in serious danger of a giant explosion, as the hippies and greasers began fighting each other every day in the quad, it was Richard whom the principal turned to to solve the problem. Which he did, in a way that ended with the student leaders themselves, with a little help from Richard, finding a permanent peace.

Day after day I watched him closely and tried to absorb his great strengths. But, since impatience and pig-headedness lay deep in my DNA, it took Richard a number of weeks to teach me the rudiments of becoming a good teacher.

Fast forward several months, to the last hour before spring vacation. We were alone in the classroom. Richard was at his desk, grading the tail end of a large stack of student papers. I gathered up my papers and books and headed for the door. "Well," I chirped, "have a good holiday, Richard," knowing full well by this time that he was going home to a family in chaos and that he and his wife were splitting up.

"You too, Joyce," he said, knowing full well that my alcoholic husband had finally left our home and I was worried about my children.

I turned back from the door and sat down in front of him. "I love you," I said.

There was this long, long silence as he stared at me in shock. "Oh," he said. "I like you too."

I ran out of that school building, furious and embarrassed. I stood in the parking lot beating the hood of my car, getting madder and madder because the dents I made kept popping back up, and what the hell right did a goddamn second-hand Chevy have implying that my pain was weak and shallow? Then I cried all the way home.

Five days later I had a call from Richard. I felt this little twist in my chest. But what he said was, "I wonder if we might get together at my house to go over some of the work you'll be doing next week."

"Oh, OK, yeah, sure," I said.

"I have been thinking about what you told me."

"Oh?" I said.

"Yes," was all he said.

When I knocked on his door he opened it. We looked at each other. We smiled at each other. "Come in," he said. "Would you like to listen to this record I just bought of Dylan Thomas reading his poetry?"

"Uh, sure," I said.

So we listened. There was a lot of throbbing sexuality threaded through that poetry; it was Dylan Thomas. Was Richard trying to tell me something? When the record was over, all he said was, "I think he's a beautiful poet with a great voice. Do you like him?"

"Well, yes," I said, ready to choke. "I do like his poetry quite a bit, but I have to be honest and tell you that that over-the-top way he recites it, well, it just makes me want to smack him." And then, while the devil was still in me, I added, "I bet you like Robert Frost's poetry too, right?"

"I do, very much," he said quietly and I was immediately ashamed of myself because I had meant that as a little slap at all things emotionally slow, steady and stoically New England. But he didn't seem fazed.

"Would you like to go out to my garden and see my roses?" he said.

"Roses?" I said. "You grow roses? Oh, Lord, I tried growing roses for a few years. What a lot of work, always getting blackrot or whatever you call it. And I know they may look great and they do smell wonderful, but then you have to watch out for all those damn prickers when you pick them."

"Yes," he said, smiling at me, "but I think the rewards of prickly roses are worth it."

And so we went outside and it was then, and it was there, in his garden, that we both, each in our own way, began the long, long path toward discovering how much our love was very like those damn sweet-smelling, beautiful and prickly roses. Three decades of those roses it turned out to be.

A Rappahannock Tale

Last Christmas I received a card from the couple who live across the road from me. "Merry Christmas to our favorite neighbor," they wrote.

We've lived across the road from each other for 27 years. Last year was the first that that word "favorite" had ever appeared on a card from them.

Considering that for decades they have both been among

the most highly respected and prominent members of our community and that they are a couple who tend to keep their feelings to themselves, I have to admit that, while that card certainly pleased me, it also surprised me a bit. Maybe more than a bit, because, though they have been kind and generous neighbors to me for many years and they know how much I like them, I'm sure they still remember how, in the first few years we moved here to Rappahannock County, my family committed three egregious acts that in various ways and to various degrees must have made the old-timers here wonder what kind of people they had let into their good county.

Our journey into Rappahannock County began with an advertisement for a Kubota tractor. "Now available with hydrostatic drive," it said.

Those words "hydrostatic drive" changed our lives. It told my husband Richard that his being in a wheelchair with useless legs was no longer a barrier to being a farmer because he could drive that Kubota with a hand control.

We happened at the time to be living in Chevy Chase, DC. Our land consisted of a backyard that was 70 x 60 feet, maybe. We're talking here about a 19-horsepower Kubota.

Fortunately, both of us wanted a farm, though to start out with, we did have somewhat different pictures of what that meant. Richard had the larger and more realistic vision: he'd grown up on a farm and he knew a great deal about farming. And he was also the kind of guy who could always find his way around obstacles, so running a farm from a wheelchair with a wife who knew nothing about farming struck him as a reasonable sort of challenge. I, on the other hand, well, I remembered what fun it was when, as a kid, I lived out in the country with my grandparents, so of course I loved farms. But I not only knew nothing about farming, I had all my life avoided outdoor physical exercise of any kind. I also happen to be a bit dyslexic when it comes to parsing almost any kind of machinery. Nevertheless, for some unfathomable reason, I too thought farming was going to be a delightful challenge. Probably, anyway. We figured that Rappahannock County would find us pretty good people. We'd both had careers as award-winning teachers. We were hard workers. We didn't think the locals were yokels the way some city people did. Surely in no time we would become respected, community-minded, successful organic farmers.

And then came the three egregious acts.

To start off with, before we got here, the school administration had been harboring high expectations for us, especially for Richard. The *Washington Post* had just run a front-page story about him. Among other things, it reported that he and I would often take his archaeology students on digs, including one Smithsonian dig up near Front Royal, next door to Rappahannock County. It was understandable for the Rappahannock school administration to simply take for granted that we would be happy to teach archeology to the students out here for years to come.

Unfortunately, we were finished with all that. It took a little while to convince them, but finally it became pretty clear to everyone that no matter how many times parents and teachers implored us, we had every intention of letting down the younger generation of Rappahannock County.

The second of our three egregious acts was totally different. God knows, nothing like it had come close to happening to us in the big bad city where you would have expected it might happen. A murder in Rappahannock County is not a common event. But it happened to our family within the first hour of our moving here.

On that fateful first day of our life in this new and wonderful Eden, the younger of Richard's two adopted sons, my stepson Bob, a young man who had for months before we moved here come out on weekends to help his dad plant an orchard and build a shed, who loved to climb Old Rag Mountain, who had walked or driven through almost every hollow in this county, who had planned to marry a young widow he'd fallen in love with and get a job out here as an auto mechanic, but who was also still a wild child who used drugs as part of his daily diet – this young man, who was driving one of our moving vans and had nearly reached our house, this young man was shot and killed by his friend sitting next to him, a boy full of drugs that Bob had given him.

And then, a minute later, the young man who had shot Bob fled in that van so wildly down Rock Mills Road that, at a curve, he crashed into a tree and killed himself.

I've thought often about those terrible moments, how it happened but also perhaps why it happened. The obvious answer is that these two young men had taken some pretty strong drugs, but it's always felt like an incomplete answer to me. While it was devastating for our family to lose my stepson who seemed on the cusp of turning his life around, I have often thought about the mystery of the boy who shot my stepson, a handsome inner city kid with a delightful sense of humor and a big grin, but a boy who had never once, in his 19 years, stepped one foot outside of Washington DC. I'll never know what happened.

As awful and shocking as that event was to the community,

especially, I imagine, to my neighbors across the road, I sometimes wonder if, from the standpoint of the taxpayers of Rappahannock County, our third egregious act was the worst of all.

All Rappahannock citizens, admittedly some more than others, keep a close eye on how tax dollars are spent here. Our money may be spent parsimoniously but our beliefs about how our money should be spent are expressed extravagantly. So, when Richard spoke up at a Board of Supervisors meeting to tell the supervisors that they were now required by federal law to make the courthouse handicapped accessible, it was the beginning of a war between those who thought making the courthouse accessible was the right and just thing to do and those who thought it was an outrageous waste of the taxpayers' money since there were always strong men around who could haul any handicapped person upstairs anytime they needed it. A war in which Richard, in his stubborn and Quakerly way, was the winner, thus causing this county to have to spend $40,000 on one of those damn automatic climbing chairs.

By this time, I was feeling a little uncomfortable in my new home. Every time I walked into the Little Washington post office, the postmistress, who happened to be married to the chairman of the board of supervisors, would turn to another customer and loudly complain about how "some people in this county just don't care how much of our hard-earned money they think we should spend on them."

Eventually Richard and I became successful organic farmers. We sold our produce to stores and restaurants, like our county's beloved Four and Twenty Blackbirds. We taught a number of people here how to raise asparagus. We were welcomed to serve on various boards. Richard became the head of the organic certification program in the state of Virginia. I became a storyteller. We were almost, almost well and truly part of our community.

Finally, not long before Richard's death in 2002, it happened. Standing at the town's bank in the line next to me one day, our postmistress of Little Washington turned to me and, in a pleasant voice said, "Good morning, Joyce. Hasn't this been lovely weather?"

And a few years later, I got that extra-special Christmas card from my neighbors across the road.

Ah, forgiveness!

Afterword

This book had its beginnings in 1984 when I met the award-winning actress-director Julie Portman who had settled in Rappahannock County with her husband the same year that we came here. A few years later, after taking one of her life stories workshops, I was inspired to create an annual autobiographical storytelling show at our local theatre, a show I called "No Ordinary Person," featuring the life stories of our county residents as told by them. This show has been running for nearly 20 years as of this writing.

The stories here are closely based on the ones I have told over the years at the No Ordinary Person show. They are mostly stories of my childhood. I've written little about my life as a teacher, a farmer, a wife, a mother, a member of the Rappahannock community, or how things have gone since the death in 2002 of my husband, Richard Abell. I left out most stories involving people still living.

One of the main reasons I have written this book is because, in my old age, I am acutely aware of how close to me Death lies. I also know that after death most of us are quickly forgotten or, at the very least, changed so much in people's memories that there's not much of our "true" selves left to pass on to the generations after that. I can attest to how surprised I sometimes am when I happen to read today's descriptions of famous people who were alive and well in the first half of my life. I invariably wonder, when some reporter describes a certain Late Great Someone, who the devil is he talking about? I am aware there was plenty about those LGSs that I didn't know about when they were still alive, so my own picture of them is undoubtedly skewed, but all too often people from the past are described in ways that make them almost totally unrecognizable.

I understand why we forget. We want life while we can grab it and to hell with the past. I don't object. (Not that it matters if I do.) But, truth to tell, that hasn't kept me from wanting to be remembered for a while longer.

The first truly overwhelming joy in my life was giving birth to my son, Crispin Sartwell, and then having had the privilege to watch his delight in discovering and understanding his new, amazing world. Now, more than 50 years later, I realize he has never stopped. My hope is that Crispin's children, my grandchildren Emma, Sam and Jane, will read this book some day and pass it on to their children, who might pass it on to their children, forever and ever and ever.

Amen.

Joyce Abell

Joyce Abell
June, 2017

Acknowledgments

I would like to thank Kendra Kopelke and Mary Azrael for their generous praise and support of my work, as well as their prior publishing of one of my stories, "The Red Menace of Ravinia," in *Passager.* I would also like to express my appreciation to Christine Drawl for her editorial and camera deftness and Pantea Amin Tofangchi for her beautiful book design.

And, most of all, I want to express my deepest gratitude to Marion Winik, the most invincible person I know, a wonderful writer of the triumphs, sorrows and mixed-up craziness of life. She was the one who guided me, with infinite patience and competence, through the forest of words I had written, and finally beamed me up into "the light," otherwise known as the publishing world.

In legends, the crane stands for longevity, peace, harmony, good fortune and fidelity. A high flyer, it is cherished for its ability to see both heaven and earth. These ancient, magnificent birds, so crucial in the wild as an "umbrella species," are now endangered and must be protected.

Passager Books is dedicated to making public the passions of a generation vital to our survival.

If you would like to support Passager Books, please visit our website www.passagerbooks.com or email us at editors@passagerbooks.com.

Prickly Roses was designed and typeset by Pantea Amin Tofangchi using Adobe InDesign. The pages are set in Adobe Garamond Pro.

Printed in 2017 by Spencer Printing, Honesdale, PA.

Also from Passager Books

A Cartography of Peace
Jean L. Connor

Improvise in the Amen Corner
Larnell Custis Butler

A Little Breast Music
Shirley J. Brewer

A Hinge of Joy
Jean L. Connor

Everything Is True at Once
Bart Galle

Perris, California
Norma Chapman

Nightbook
Steve Matanle

I Shall Go As I Came
Ellen Kirvin Dudis

Keeping Time:
150 Years of Journal Writing
edited by Mary Azrael and Kendra Kopelke

Burning Bright:
Passager Celebrates 21 Years
edited by Mary Azrael and Kendra Kopelke

Hot Flash Sonnets
Moira Egan

Beyond Lowu Bridge
Roy Cheng Tsung

Because There Is No Return
Diana Anhalt

Never the Loss of Wings
Maryhelen Snyder

The Want Fire
Jennifer Wallace

Little Miracles
James K. Zimmerman

View from the Hilltop
A Collection by The North Oaks Writers
edited by Barbara Sherr Roswell and Christine Drawl

The Chugalug King & Other Stories
Andrew Brown

Gathering the Soft
Becky Dennison Sakellariou
Paintings by Tandy Zorba

Finding Mr. Rightstein
Nancy Davidoff Kelton

The Three O'Clock Bird
Anne Frydman

A Sunday in Purgatory
Henry Morgenthau III